Hosea
and His Message

Roy L. Honeycutt

BROADMAN PRESS
Nashville, Tennessee

1,50
6

All Scripture quotations are from the Revised Standard Version, unless otherwise indicated.

Scripture quotations marked NEB are from *The New English* Bible.

Dewey Decimal Classification: 224.6
Library of Congress Catalog Card Number: 74-33075
Printed in the United States of America

Contents

1

The Valley of Tears

1:1 to 3:5

Alienation, separation, estrangement; each of these suggests the brokenness which characterizes life. Throughout the Bible separation and alienation are common themes to describe both man's sin and his suffering. Whether for a primal couple, Adam and Eve, who epitomize man's alienation from God (Gen. 3:1 ff), or for Hosea whose separation from his wife is lifted into the canon of Scripture to illustrate God's suffering in response to man's separation; brokenness and alienation are life's constant companions.

The grief of Hosea's marital crisis was so shattering as to constitute a "valley of tears" through which the prophet passed. So like the suffering of Jesus was that of Hosea that H. Wheeler Robinson once characterized the prophet's experience as "The Cross of Hosea." The domestic tragedy through which Hosea passed was his valley of tears. But it was more. It became the vehicle which enabled Hosea to see that through his suffering and tears there shone the light of a love imperishable. Such love not only transcended his suffering, it transformed his suffering. It filled suffering with meaning, reflecting in it the matchless love of God for alienated, separated, lost persons who, as surely as ever Gomer abandoned Hosea, abandon the Lord.

Through the dark shadows of his valley of tears, Hosea experienced as have few others divine qualities of both suffering and love. He saw reflected in the face of his own suffering a cross in the heart of God, suggesting both the suffering and the love with which God responded to man's faithlessness.

Thus, Hosea's broken marriage, so graphically described in the opening chapters of the book, became for him and for successive believers within the community of faith the occasion for God's revelation of a love that transcends lovelessness, of a loyalty that is greater than faithlessness, of a wholeness that can transform brokenness.

The first three chapters of Hosea are bound together by a common theme: the separation and reunion of Hosea and Gomer. Within the framework of those chapters there are diverse literary forms from different periods of time. But the unity of the common theme transcends the diversity of the separate units. The disciple who arranged the book in its present form wove the diversities of the first three chapters into a single focus: the disintegration and ultimate restoration of Hosea's marriage. There are three major sub-themes in chapters 1 to 3, each dynamically related to the broader theme. These sub-themes are: (1) the cross of revelation (1:1 to 2:1), (2) the course of infidelity (2:2-23), and (3) the compassion that is born of God (3:1-5).

I. The Cross of Revelation, 1:1 to 2:1

To affirm that biblical religion is a "religion of history" is to affirm that God reveals himself through specific, historical events. While revelation does come through "word," there is an interlocking relationship between "word" and "deed" which cannot be ignored without running risks of oversimplification and misunderstanding. These risks concern both the nature of the biblical revelation and the manner in which God reveals himself in contemporary settings.

Revelation does not come through the suspension of the historical order and the faculties of man, but through an appropriate intensification and interpretation of those factors. Biblical revelation affirms that God responds to man in the throes of his struggles. Hosea's experiences became a means whereby God revealed himself as "suffering love." Quite significantly, it was not in Hosea's withdrawal from the crushing events of life that God spoke to the prophet. Rather, it was in the context of his broken home that the prophet perceived the revelation of God.

For Hosea, revelation in history came in three ways: through personal crisis (1:2-3), through symbolic action, the naming of the children (1:4-9), and through prophetic interpretation of history (1:10 to 2:1).

1. Revelation Through Personal Crisis, 1:2-3

Suffering and crisis were not merely attendant to the Lord's revelation through Hosea. They were the means of revelation. As in the case of Jesus, suffering was the vehicle of revelation. It formed the medium of his ministry; it was not merely an accompaniment to ministry. He achieved the purposes of his life through suffering. So, in the case of Hosea, the revelation of God was achieved *through* the personal anguish and heartbreak attendant to his broken family.

That Hosea's marriage was revelatory is clearly implied in the statement "the LORD said to Hosea" (v. 2). As the prophet interpreted his marriage, he saw that it was within the providence of God that he married Gomer, unfaithful though she was.

First, the marriage of Gomer was itself a revelation of love. "Take to yourself a wife of harlotry" is subject to a variety of interpretations. Many are convinced that Gomer was not a harlot at the time of the marriage, that Hosea is speaking in retrospect when he says that the Lord said for him to marry a harlot. According to this view, Gomer was virtuous at the time of marriage, but destined to become a harlot. Such a view is maintained largely because of the difficulty of reconciling the command to marry a harlot with what is understood to be the moral character of God. Hence, some have interpreted the statement allegorically, and an early Jewish commentator, Ibn Ezra, interpreted the entire scene as having occurred in a vision.

It appears the better part of wisdom, however, to take the passage quite literally, despite difficulties which this may precipitate for one's view of the nature of God. According to this position, Gomer was at the time of the marriage a "harlot." Whether she was a common prostitute, as some suggest, or a cultic prostitute associated with the worship of Baal, a Canaanite deity, is difficult to determine. The probability is that she was a young woman who had participated in the fertility rites associated with Canaanite religion; Baalism being a primary concern of the book of Hosea (cf. 2:6-8,16).

On one occasion a student protested vigorously such an interpretation of the Lord's command to Hosea that he marry Gomer. "How," he asked, "could God ever command a prophet to marry a prostitute or one who had participated in sexual rites related to Baalism?" Yet, what greater demonstration is there of the reality of a love that transcends our own than that Hosea should do precisely this: respond with genuine love and affection to such a young woman and, in accord with his understanding of the will of God, marry her? Is not this so very much like the love of God for us "while we were yet sinners"? The command to marry a harlot is a revelation of that quality of unmerited love which is characteristic of God's love.

A *second* revelatory aspect of Hosea's marriage is the crisis precipitated by the unfaithfulness of Gomer and her apparent abandonment of both Hosea and her children (cf. 2:2 ff).

Just as there are few metaphors more descriptive of the ideal relationship between the Lord and his people than that of marriage, so there are fewer more graphic ways of describing the faithlessness and estrangement of the people of God than to describe them metaphorically as adultery. The book of Hosea should be read with bifocal vision. One part of one's vision should focus upon Hosea and Gomer. The other part of one's vision should focus upon the Lord and Israel. Out of the agony of his own suffering and the bitter disappointment of his broken marriage and family, Hosea came to see that Israel had responded in like manner to the Lord. Confused about the true source of her provisions and blessings, Israel ascribed to the Canaanite fertility god, Baal, those blessings which had come ultimately from the Lord.

In retrospect, it is difficult for some to understand how this may have happened. Yet it happens continually. When persons move from one cultural era to another, just as Israel moved from one way of life to another in moving from the fringes of the desert to the settled farms of Canaan, there is always the subtle temptation to abandon the Lord of the past for new gods of the culture into which one has entered. This is the continuing, fundamental question for every generation: Is the God of yesterday adequate for the crises of today?

Through the sorrow of his own suffering Hosea saw that Israel had abandoned the Lord just as Gomer had abandoned her husband and children. But more than this, Hosea came to understand that

God suffers in response to estrangement and alienation just as a husband does when he is forsaken by his wife. Yet still more, Hosea came to see that this suffering was accompanied by an imperishable love, that the Lord never ceases to love his people despite the suffering etched into his heart.

2. Revelation Through Symbolic Action, 1:4-9

Names, for those of us in the twentieth century, are basically no more than a means of distinguishing one person from another. But for persons of the biblical era names were fraught with significance. The name was the summation of the person. For example, the name of Jacob was changed to Israel on the occasion of his meeting the Lord at Penuel. He had been changed; hence his name was changed. Or, consider the significance of the son described by Isaiah: "She . . . shall call his name Immanuel" (Isa. 7:14). The name of this child signified the unique presence of God: "God with us" was his name. Or consider the name of Jesus: "You shall call his name Jesus, for he will save his people from their sins" (Mat. 1:21). "Jesus" comes from a root word which means "to save"; hence, his name summarizes his function. So, names could be used as signs, as ways of communicating some great action or meaning on the part of God.

In the names given to his children, Hosea sought to convey specific insight into God's action with his people. Not only do the names suggest Hosea's action toward Gomer, they also suggest the Lord's action against his "wife," Israel. In this regard, the action of Hosea is like that of Isaiah later in the same century. Isaiah also gave strange names to his children, suggesting the fate of Israel: "Shearjashub" (Isa. 7:3), implying that "a remnant shall return," and "Mahershalal-hashbaz" which literally means "the spoil speeds, the prey hastens"—that is, the day of reckoning is hastening on for the people of God. Although this action is relatively strange in contemporary circles, it was common in the Old Testament. Names conveyed meanings beyond themselves, often awesome meanings.

Three children were born to Gomer, and with each successive child Hosea used a name suggesting the alienation of those who had betrayed God's love and fidelity. In the use of the name "Jezreel," which means "God sows or scatters," Hosea declared that the line of Jehu had come to an end in the death of Zechariah, son of Jeroboam killed at Ibleam (vv. 4-5).

The second child, a daughter (vv. 6 ff), was named "Lo-ruchamah" which means "Not pitied." No longer will the Lord have pity upon those who betray the bonds of their relationship. There is an end to the patience of God. In response to faithlessness and infidelity, compassion is turned aside for the moment and men are given over to the fruit of their own actions.

The last child of the prophet and his wife, a son, was named "Lo-ami"—literally, "not my people." Whether the name is intended to suggest that the child was not Hosea's is debatable, but there is no doubt that the use of the name is the prophet's means of saying that Israel has broken the covenant relationship. In the Old Testament, generally, the clause "I will be your God and you shall be my people" is a way of describing the warmth of the covenant relationship. Here, that relationship has been shattered, although in response to the initial unfaithfulness of Israel.

How graphically did Hosea describe the inevitable results of Israel's faithlessness, of the faithlessness of any generation that abandons the Lord. In response to the infidelity to covenant bonds, the Lord is about to scatter the dynastic line of Jehu, the reigning dynasty at the initiation of Hosea's ministry. The Lord is no longer to have pity ("Lo-ruchamah"). Those who have been called his people are no longer to be known as the people of God. They are "Lo-ami"— "not my people."

In this strange but vivid manner, the prophet describes the inevitable result of abandoning one's relationship with the Lord. The stability of the kingly dynasty is to disintegrate. No longer is life to be characterized by "pity." The most treasured relationship one can have, that personal and dynamic relationship with the Lord, is to pass away. In these ways Hosea describes the fleeting, disappointing nature of life characterized by infidelity to one's relationship with the Lord.

3. Revelation Through Prophetic Interpretation, 1:10 to 2:1

Revelation also comes through the inspired interpretation of history which a prophet may bring to a situation. The interpretation of "what's happening to you" is a primary means of revelation. Against the background of one's relationship with the Lord, how do you understand these events? Hosea saw in the unfolding events of the future a time when the apostasy and infidelity of that present moment would be replaced by faithfulness and devotion. His interpretation is couched in words which are deliberately contrary to the names used for the children. For example, in naming his first child "Jezreel," Hosea affirmed that the Lord would scatter Israel (vv. 4-5). Here the prophet insists that the time will come when, figuratively speaking, the people of Israel cannot be numbered. Those who were scattered have somehow multiplied into a number beyond compare.

In the same manner, Hosea spoke of that time when positive features of the relationship between Israel and the Lord would counteract those previous statements. For example, he previously had named his daughter "Lo-ruchamah" in order to suggest an end to the pity of God. But he believed that the time would come when "Lo-ruchamah" would be called "Ruchamah": "She has obtained pity" (2:1). In the same manner, the name of the last son, "Lo-ami" ("not my people"), will someday be changed to "Ami" ("my people"), suggesting that those who once were not the people of God are now his people.

What is suggested through the reversal which characterizes each of these three names? Perhaps there is no better way to answer this than in the words of Abraham Heschel who once said, "No word is God's last word." God always has one more word for guilty sinners. That word is always one of grace and love, of reconciliation and wholeness, of comfort and peace.

This pattern is characteristic of Hosea, as of other biblical writers. Following messages of doom there are messages of hope. Just as in this instance, so at the conclusion of chapter 2, the theme is one of restoration and renewal. Also, the final chapter closes with an emphasis upon reconciliation and return to the Lord. In this connection it may be noted that while major discussions of Hosea's marital experiences most often focus upon infidelity and abandonment on the part of Gomer, the climax of the experience is the loving action of Hosea which lead to the return of Gomer (3:1 ff). Hosea's last word is one of grace and restoration. For those of us caught in the complicity and the sin of our own action, it may strengthen and encourage us to remember that this is still the way of God. God's last word is always one of restoration, forgiveness, and reconciliation.

So, in summary, Hosea's cross became a means of revelation. Through the suffering of numerous disappointments and heartbreak, he came to see with greater clarity the outlines of God's purposes. Revelation came through specific deeds, just as it does today. God is seeking to speak to us in our own multiple crises. Revelation came to Hosea through personal crisis (vv. 2-3), through symbolic names given his children (vv. 4-9), and through his own inspired interpretation of the nature of God's action in reversing the infidelity and faithlessness of man (1:10 to 2:1).

II. The Course of Infidelity, 2:2-23

Hosea allegorizes his own experience, seeing in it a reflection of Israel's experience with the Lord. His suffering and anguish with Gomer became a pattern or shadow of another quality of suffering and anguish which the Lord knew in his relationship with his people. Hosea described the fact of infidelity (2:2-5), the consequences of infidelity (2:6-15), and the way in which grace responds to infidelity (2:16-23). Has the course which infidelity runs greatly changed? Are we caught in the same quality of infidelity in our relationship with the Lord as was ancient Israel, as Gomer was with Hosea? Have the consequences greatly changed in principle? Does God continue to respond in grace, despite our infidelity? The chapter at hand affirms appropriate yes and no answers to each of these questions.

1. The Fact of Infidelity, 2:2-5

In a passage strikingly like descriptions of actual divorce scenes of the ancient Near East, Hosea described the expulsion of Gomer, together with the clear statement of charges against her: "Their mother has played the harlot; she that conceived them has acted shamefully" (v. 5). Such a life of infidelity as that described by Hosea is characterized by both estrangement (v. 2) and desolation (vv. 3-5).

The *estrangement* or separation of man from God is always one facet of his infidelity. The loneliness and solitude which haunt those who lose touch with God who is the source of meaning, community, and life are graphically characterized by the prophet. Are there more haunting words than these: "She is not mine, and I am not hers" (v. 2)? Sin always separates. It results in brokenness and estrangement. Sin sets in motion an eternal sadness characteristic of those who wander throughout life in loneliness and isolation. How tragic when Hosea's words to Gomer (v. 2) are appropriately transposed to describe our relationship to the Lord: "He is not mine, and I am not his" (cf. v. 2).

Renunciation is a second aspect of infidelity.

Having formally declared that Gomer is no longer his wife (v. 2), Hosea renounces her, stripping away all that she has, making her "as in the day she was born" (v. 3). Yet more than Gomer is involved. A nation is involved. I am involved—together with you. For Hosea affirms that all we have we owe to God. What would we have should he demand the return of all that he has given? Would we not, figuratively, be "naked . . . as in the day she was born . . . like a wilderness . . . a parched land"? Later, Hosea is to say even more specifically, "I will take back" (2:9). How poverty stricken would we be should he take back all that he has given: health, mind, energy, purpose, meaning, hope, destiny, eternal life—take it all back!

2. The Consequences of Infidelity, 2:6-15

The Hebrew particle *ki'*, "therefore," appears three times in successive verses (vv. 6,9,14) and has been used by the author of the book to indicate three basic consequences of such infidelity as that characterized in Hosea.

First, futility characterizes infidelity, (vv. 6-8). Reminiscent of biblical passages which speak of those who hunger but are not filled, who thirst but remain unsatisfied, Hosea suggests that Israel will pursue but not overtake her lovers. She will "seek them, but shall not find them" (v. 7). How like the unfulfilled desires of contemporary persons: individuals who appear to have everything but who have nothing that brings genuine satisfaction. To a restless, searching, unsatisfied generation, the words of Hosea are uniquely appropriate: Failure to live out a dynamic relationship with God and with the community of faith brings an accompanying lack of ultimate satisfaction.

Exposed to the meaninglessness and futility of life apart from the Lord, Israel comes to her senses. She decides that she will return to her "first husband," the Lord, as opposed to the Canaanite Baal who is her lover (v. 7). Realizing that it was "better with me then than now" (v. 7), she decides upon a return to the Lord. She had compounded her error, however, by having ascribed to Baal blessings which the Lord provided (v. 8). Little did she know that throughout her adultery and infidelity, it was the Lord who continued to provide the "grain, the wine, and the oil" which she had ascribed to the Canaanite interloper, Baal.

Do we have the same myopic vision which causes us to ascribe to contemporary gods of our own making—whether they are scientific technology or human ingenuity—those blessings which come ultimately from the Lord? Admitted that scientific technology as well as creative, human ingenuity are prerequisite to the many and bountiful achievements which are ours in contemporary society. Have we seen clearly enough when we fail to recognize that beyond all of our technology and ingenuity there stands the Lord of the universe, unnoticed but dynamically responsible for all that we have? To state it otherwise, are we actually so greatly different from Israel of Hosea's day who mistakenly ascribed the gifts of God to the nature deity, Baal, rather than to the Lord of history, Yahweh?

Second, infidelity leads to a *forsaken* quality of life (vv. 9-13). The products of the natural order—grain, wine, flax, etc.—were thought by Canaanites worshiping Baal, and by Israelites who succumbed to that worship or who introduced elements of Baalism into the worship of Yahweh, to have been the gifts of Baal. Through sexual rites associated with fertility cults generally and with Baalism more specifically, worshipers believed it possible to unite cosmic procreative powers. The release of such procreative power assured the fecundity of field and flock, of vineyard and orchard. Failing to understand that the Lord provided all gifts of the natural order, Israel ascribed them to Baal.

The consequences of this are clear. The Lord will take back "my grain in its time, and my wine in its season; and I will take away my wool and my flax, which were to cover her nakedness" (v. 9). Israel's festive and sometimes sexually-oriented feasts will be put to an end (v. 11). The "hire" given to the prostitute is to be taken from her (Israel); suggesting that the bounty Israel ascribed to Baal was essentially the price of her prostitution (v. 12).

Upon reading the narrative we are quick to condemn ancient Israel: condemning her for mistakenly ascribing to nature deities, who were personifications of various powers in nature, those gifts which come from the Lord. We understand and affirm the clear analogy between her action and that of a prostitute who sells herself for the material gift of the moment in lieu of a continuing, dynamic, and personal relationship grounded in "love." Yet, are we so far removed from the possibility of such action in our own generation?

Forgetting the ultimate source of our bounty, ravaging the earth for the sake of ourselves in the Western world, do we also run the risk of losing the bounty which we have known? May not history judge us as Hosea did his own generation? Is there a sense in which the natural resources which we have squandered in satisfying our own exalted standards of living become the "hire" that has lead us to forsake long-term, dynamic, and personal relationships with the Lord and other persons in exchange for the fleeting gratification of the moment? To use the language of Hosea, have we prostituted ourselves in our relationships with both the Lord and the larger, human family? Hosea affirms that the "hire" of the harlot, Gomer, is to be taken from her. Under any stretch of the imagination are we justified in assuming that we shall be exempt in those same areas for which Israel stood accountable before God?

Third, it is precisely at this juncture, at the depth of degradation and need, that the Lord injects the possibility of *forgiveness* and *reconciliation,* the hope of a new beginning and a renewal of those earlier dynamic relationships which Israel shared with the Lord during the "honeymoon" experienced in the wilderness following the Exodus (2:1 ff; 14-15). As suggested previously, "no word is God's last word," especially when that word is spoken in the context of judgment and condemnation. God's last word is always one of forgiveness and restoration. One should maintain the proper tension

between the *wrath in God's love* and the *love in God's wrath*, but
in so doing let us continue through wrath and judgment to forgiveness
and restoration. Any proclamation of judgment in history, as needed
as that is and as appropriate as that may be, which stops short of
announcing the possibility of forgiveness and reconciliation is not
yet "good news," gospel.

Throughout several books of the prophets the wilderness is looked
upon as an ideal period, what some moderns would term a "honeymoon" (cf. Jer. 2:1 ff; Ezek. 16:8 ff). Looking toward the future
hope for the people of God, prophets interpreted that hope on
occasion in terms of a "new exodus" (cf. Ezek. 20:32-38; Isa. 40:1
ff). In Isaiah 40—55 alone there are at least ten passages which
speak of the hope of God's people in terms of a "new exodus"—of
a time when the old exodus will not merely be repeated, but when
God is to bring about a new exodus which will transcend the old.
Even in the New Testament vocabulary used to describe the saving
work of Christ is drawn from the Exodus: "redeem," "redemption,"
"deliver," "ransom," "purchase," "bondage," "freedom." Also, in
Pauline thought alone there are in all about forty references or
allusions to the history of the Exodus. Hosea stands as the wellspring
of this reinterpretation of the Exodus.

Thus, the hope expressed in verse 14 is part of a larger hope,
an eschatological hope: Someday, God will lead his people once
again into that place where he can speak tenderly to them. We
await with anticipation that day, just as the community of faith
has waited with hope across the centuries. But it is not easy to return
to that place where God can speak tenderly to you, to that place
where the names of the false gods can be removed from our lips
(v. 17), so that we can speak the name of One who stands in true
relationship with his people (vv. 16-17).

What is the significance of "the valley of Achor" (v. 15)? Where
was it? What was the significance of the name? The "valley of Achor"
stood between conquering Israel and the Promised Land. It was
through this valley that she proceeded in her march from Jericho
to the highlands of Canaan (cf. Josh. 7:1 ff; especially v. 24). The
valley was "a door of hope" in that it was the doorway that lead

to the Promised Land.

But more than its role as a doorway leading to the Promised Land
is implied in the reference to the valley of Achor as a "door of
hope." It was in the valley of Achor that Achan was judged for
his sin in precipitating Israel's failure to take the city of Ai (Josh.
7:2 ff). Because of his violation of the "ban," which precluded the
secular use of the plunder from Jericho, Achan and his entire family
were put to death (Josh. 7:16 ff). It was in that valley that Achan
and his family were judged. Israel "stoned him with stones; . . .
and they raised over him a great heap of stones that remains to
this day" (vv. 25-26). According to the writer (Josh. 7:26), it was
for that reason that the valley was called "valley of Achor"—which
means "valley of trouble."

The door of hope so often lies beyond the valley of trouble! Hosea
probably had in mind the judgment that Israel inevitably was to
experience in the eighth century, B.C. Hope lay beyond judgment.
Such an attitude rests on far more than a Pollyanna attitude which
suggests that "it is always darkest before the storm." Before there
can be hope, there *must* be judgment. But judgment without hope
is a distortion of the biblical posture of both judgment and hope.

Not only so, some persons (perhaps all of us) must be driven through
the extremity of circumstance—our own "valley of trouble"—to the
point that we are ready to return. Hosea affirms that return and
renewal involve more than a glib, superficial expression of intention.
In the agony and suffering of trouble, akin to Hosea's experience
with Gomer and so much like the suffering of Israel in history,
believers are led to perceive a door of hope lying always just beyond
their valley of trouble. This is a part of what it means to believe
in the grace of God. Without such hope could we know anything
other than meaningless despair? Thank God for the valley of trouble
that is prerequisite to a newborn hope. Equally thankful are those
caught in the valley of trouble but who see beyond to a door of
hope. With this interpretation of life one can both face and triumph
over whatever life may bring.

3. Grace Responds to Infidelity, 2:16-23

There will come a day when the Lord will make a "new covenant"

with his people (cf. Jer. 31:31; Matt. 26:26 f). Probably written after
the ravages of Tiglath-Pileser III in approximately 733 B.C., the
passage speaks of the way in which God does bring hope beyond
the valley of trouble. Three identical phrases, "in that day," introduce
three distinct and separate emphases (vv. 16,18,21).

What is the day of the new covenant to be like, that day when
the Lord acts anew in the life of a returning people? *First*, it will
be a day when we will learn again to speak the name of God with
appropriate love and devotion. Israel had apparently begun to worship Baal or, more likely, had begun to corrupt the worship of God
with elements of Baalism. The word "Baal" means lord in the sense
of a local master over a given territory. Through corrupted practices,
Israel had begun to call Yahweh "Baal." "In that day" Israel will
call the Lord *ishi*, my man or my husband; not *baali*, my Baal or
"lord" in the Canaanite sense. That the way we speak of God, in
the sense that it is the bringing to reality of our conceptions and
identifications of God, is of ultimate significance is reflected in the
fact that the Third Commandment speaks specifically to the use
of the name of God. Through the grace of God himself, which is
not isolated from judgment in history, we will someday come to
the point that he will "remove the names of the Baals" (v. 17) from
our mouths. It is an action that he will accomplish. Such a day
will be a day of new loyalty.

Second, that day of the new covenant will be a time of new
beginnings for the whole of the created order. That the covenant
is not merely local is suggested in the statement, "I will make for
you a covenant on that day with the beasts of the field, the birds
of the air" (v. 18). Note the similarity between the "beasts,"
"birds," "creeping things" and the creation narrative of Genesis 1:1
ff. It is to be a universal covenant, a time when the whole of creation
symbolically returns to its primal beginnings. It will be a time of
peace, unlike the ravages of Assyria. It shall be a time when persons
may "lie down in safety" (v. 18). Such a covenant will bring a new
depth of relationship with the Lord, with a new quality of duration:
". . . betroth you to me forever." Those qualities of relationship
ideally associated with covenant life shall become real: qualities of

"righteousness," "justice," "steadfast love," "mercy," "faithfulness," knowledge of the Lord. In that day, these shall be effective and real in history.

Third, that new day will be a time of new, harmonious relationship. In rhythmic harmony the whole of creation shall resound and respond to the Lord. In poetic form the prophet shares his inspired conviction that harmony shall replace disharmony, that order shall replace chaos, that rhythm shall displace dissonance. The Lord will speak and all creation shall answer; each facet of creation answering in light of its intended purpose.

But more than this, in such a time broken relationships shall be restored. Hosea returns to the polarity of meaning associated with the names of the children. Jezreel ("God sows") shall be sown on the land; whereas earlier Hosea had spoken of the breaking of Jezreel, the disintegration of the dynasty. The warmth of the relationships sustained with the Lord "in that day" is clearly reflected in Hosea's closing words: "I will have pity on Not pitied, and I will say to Not my people, 'You are my people'; and he shall say, 'Thou art my God.'" Returning to a previous theme, those who now say "He is not mine, and I am not his" (v. 23; cf. p. 11) will be able to say in that day of new relationships, "He is mine, and I am his."

III. Compassion That Is Born of God, 3:1-5

The relationship between events recorded in chapters 1 and 2 and the event described in chapter 3 is the subject of varied conclusions. As presently arranged, chapter 3 seems to record the sequel to the divorce described earlier. Others, however, have seen in chapter 3 the biographical account of the same event that is recorded in autobiographical terms in chapter 1. Again, some interpret the events recorded in chapter 3 as having occurred after the original marriage, but suggest that the woman is a person other than Gomer. The position taken here, and one that appears to be the most natural interpretation of the text as presently arranged in the book of Hosea, is that chapter 3 describes the return of Gomer out of harlotry and slavery.

Hans Walter Wolff, a German scholar, once suggested that chapter

3 of Hosea focuses on the theme, "How the Lord's Love Works." The chapter describes the effects of a love conceived in relationship with the Lord, together with an appropriate emphasis upon the nature of divine love itself. Again, one should read with bifocal vision, seeing both the love that characterizes God himself and the love in man created by a dynamic relationship with God. Elsewhere, the present writer has characterized the qualities of love reflected in chapter 3 as a love that controls (v. 1), a love that redeems (v. 2), a love that disciplines (v. 3), a love that triumphs (vv. 4-5).[1]

First, such love as prompted Hosea to redeem Gomer is conceived in the union of man's relationship with divine love. Which stands prior, Hosea's love for Gomer, or God's love for Israel? Did Hosea first love Gomer and then conclude that in a comparable way God also loved Israel? An appropriate emphasis upon the phrase "even as the LORD loves the people of Israel" (v. 1) suggests that Hosea's redemptive action originated in the exemplary love of God. Not only do we love him (God) because he first loved us; we also love others as we do because he first loved us. Love begets love.

Second, compassion and love conceived in the union of our relationship with God lead us to redemptive actions of reconciliation in our interpersonal relationships. In paying the redemption price of Gomer from slavery (v. 2), Hosea demonstrated the redeeming, reconciling nature of godly love.

Third, as Wheeler Robinson once said, "love is neither blind, nor is it weak." Hence, it should occasion no surprise that the return of Gomer involved discipline and demonstrated fidelity (v. 3). Verse 3 probably speaks of purification rites, but in any event the passage underscores Hosea's realistic attitude in his redemptive action. Gomer is set aside "for many days" and in this period of mutual sexual abstinence both the prophet and his estranged wife are witnesses to a time of trial, perhaps of demonstrated virtue.

Such an element of judgment is also applicable to Israel, and Hosea concludes by affirming that Israel also must be separated for a time without "king or prince, without sacrifice or pillar, without

---

[1] Roy L. Honeycutt, "Hosea" *The Broadman Bible Commentary*, Vol. VII, 1972.

ephod or teraphim" (v. 4). The removal of kingship and those elements associated with worship—sacrifice, pillar (marking a sacred
site), ephod, or teraphim (both of which were primitive means of
revelation)—has the collective impact of speaking to a period of
exile when Israel would no longer have access to the established
order suggested by the institutions of kingship and worship. Sin sets
in motion negative consequences (judgment) which must be experienced in route to restoration. With a love that is neither blind nor
weak, principles of moral retribution wring from every wayward
people the consequences of their sin.

Fourth, the last word is love not wrath, grace not judgment, return
not exile. Both the marriage and the divorce of Gomer are of crucial
significance in understanding divine qualities of love and suffering.
But equally important are compassion and restoration. As the author
of Hosea utilized the available information related to Hosea and
Gomer, he used the restoration motif as the climax for the entire
literary complex. Through this means of editing the material which
lay at hand, an action not unrelated to the presence of the Spirit
of God and what is normally described as "inspiration," the last
word in the Hosea-Gomer episode became one of grace and love.
Such love triumphs over faithlessness and infidelity to such a marked
degree as to lead to a renewed relationship between man and God.
This remains the continuing hope of man and the abiding message
of the Hosea-Gomer experience: love conceived in the heart of God
triumphs over faithlessness and broken relationships. Further, God's
love is expressed toward each of us so that wayward though we
may have been, God leads us in his love to experience restoration
and renewal. With love like this, we are born again to a new and
living hope.

2

The Accuser and the Accused

4:1-19

The announcement of the prophetic messenger introduces the lawsuit or controversy motif in the book of Hosea: "The LORD has a controversy with the inhabitants of the land" (v. 1). The dominant picture in "controversy" narratives is that of the heavenly assembly serving as a court of law, a portrait common to prophetic thought. The prophet understood himself not only as one who had heard what went on in the heavenly council but as a messenger of the court to announce its verdict. For example, Jeremiah affirmed of prophets in his day, "If they had stood in my council, then they would have proclaimed my words to my people" (Jer. 23:22; cf. also 23:18). Prophets have unique access to divine counsel, and they function as messengers to announce the verdict, or the "word of the LORD."

The lawsuit theme is introduced in Hosea by the word "controversy," a noun which also appears in Hosea 12:3 as well as Micah 6:2. The verbal form appears in Hosea 2:4; 4:4; Amos 7:4; Micah 6:1; and 7:9. Thus, chapter 4 introduces a distinctly new element in the book of Hosea. Having charged Israel with adulterous conduct, the prophet then specified those evidences which substantiated his initial indictment. Chapters 4—14 consist of accusations related to ways in which both religious infidelity and political irresponsibility characterized Israel's relationships with the Lord.

Specifically, chapter 4 focuses on *the accuser*, the Lord (vv. 1-3) and *the accused*, Israel (vv. 4:14; 15-19). The role of the Lord as accuser and the bases for his indictment are specifically clarified in verses 1-3. Protests of that indictment are immediately overthrown by evidence comprised of actions by both the priests (vv. 4-10) and the people (vv. 11-14).

I. Reasons for the Lord's Controversy with His People, 4:1-3

Verses 1-3 consist of a "judgment speech" (cf. Isa. 1:18 ff; 3:13 ff; Mic. 6:1-5) in which there is the announcement by the prophet who functions as a messenger, verse 1; the indictment or accusation which sets forth the bases for the controversy, verses 1-2, and the verdict or announcement of judgment, verse 3.

1. Breaking Relationship with the Lord, 4:1

That Israel had broken her relationship with the Lord is evident from the description of the positive bases for the Lord's accusation which appear in verse 1. Each of these words is uniquely related to covenant relationship: faithfulness, kindness, knowledge (of God). "Faithfulness" (*'emeth*) suggests dependability or "good faith" (NEB). It is a word directly related to the word "truth"—truth being that which is dependable. Reliability is another synonym which may clarify the meaning of the word. "Kindness" (RSV) fails to convey an appropriately dynamic denotation of the word (*chesedh*). The word describes that quality of love, sometimes called "covenant love," which precipitates loyalty to the covenant relationship. "Faithful love" conveys the appropriate meaning of the word; or, as *The New English Bible* suggests "mutual trust." The word is one of the Hebrew words for love and is used within the framework of those who stand in covenant relationship. A measure of ambiguity is present in the translator's way of translating (RSV) this word in Hosea. The identically same word (*chesedh*) is translated in these ways: "kindness" (4:1), "love" (6:4), and "steadfast love" (6:6). The word connotes faithful love within a covenant relationship.

Finally, Hosea affirmed that there was "no knowledge of God." Such knowledge is experiential, not merely intellectual. Where there is covenant relationship which is dynamic, viable, and legitimate, there will be reliability or faithfulness, steadfast love, and an appropriate experiential knowledge of God. Where these are lacking, one may rightly ask whether there is any longer any dynamic covenant relationship.

Another evidence that the covenant relationship with the Lord had been broken may be seen in Israel's fidelity or lack of fidelity to the Ten Commandments. The Decalogue is most often known in the Old Testament as the "ten words," but on occasion, that collection is known simply as "the covenant" (cf. Ex. 34:28; Deut. 4:13; 9:9). Such a designation probably arose out of the close relationship between the Commandments and covenantal responsibilities. They so summarized the demand of God that they could be spoken of as "his covenant" (Deut. 4:13) or "the tables of the covenant" (Deut. 9:9). Hosea cites specific areas of interpersonal relationships related to the Decalogue that have been violated: "Swearing, lying, killing, stealing, and committing adultery" (v. 2). The fracture of one's relationship with other persons is indicative of a fractured relationship with the Lord. The two areas of relationship are so intertwined that the one reflects the other—human and divine. The cumulative nature of their action is suggestively noted in the phrase: "they break all bounds and murder follows murder" (v. 2), or "one deed of blood after another" (NEB).

2. Broken Relationships with the Land, 4:3

Broken relationships with the Lord have as one consequence broken relationships in other areas of man's existence, in this instance with the land. Within biblical literature there is a consistent emphasis upon the interlocking nature of man and the natural order. The positive relationship of man with God and with other persons is matched by a positive relationship with the earth. Righteousness is linked to the bounty of the earth. Conversely, man's sin in some way was thought to bring about negative experiences related to the natural order. For example, in the primal context of Genesis 3, the ground itself shares in the curse (vv. 17 f). For Cain as well, "When you till the ground, it shall no longer yield to you its strength" (Gen. 4:12). Paul suggested much later that the entire creation waits "with eager longing" for the time when it "will be set free from its bondage to decay" (cf. Rom. 8:19 ff). Prophets consistently interpreted drought, earthquake, blight, and other "natural calamities" as expressions of God's judgment (cf. Amos 4:6 ff; Jer. 14:2 ff). Hosea's reference to the drought may reflect the same awesome experience as described in the vision of Amos (cf. Amos 7:4 ff; 4:7 ff). In any event, life functions with such rhythm and syncopation that if one aspect of a person's life is disrupted, other parts are also affected.

So, a broken relationship with the Lord has awesome effects for the life of man (vv. 1-2).

II. Responsibility for Apostasy and Immorality, 4:4-14

As though to hush any protest of innocence, Hosea insists: "Let no one contend, and let none accuse" (v. 4). There is no ground for excuse; the Lord's contention is with the priests (vv. 4-10) *and* the people (vv. 11-14). Hosea made use of the verb "contend" from which the noun "controversy" (v. 1) is derived. This represents a pointed and unmistakable emphasis; literally, "let no one of you contend" (v. 4)—the "contention" (v. 1) is the Lord's. He alone has any ground for argument. Only the Lord has adequate grounds for a "court of law." No one among the priests "has a case."

1. Responsibility and Guilt of Religious Leaders, 4:4-10

Intrinsic to the role of leadership is the reality of a greater level of responsibility than others may have. For example, in the reminder: "Let not many of you become teachers . . . for you know that we who teach shall be judged with greater strictness" (Jas. 3:1). A common feature of prophetic literature is the consistent manner in which prophets believe that the essential problem within the context of apostasy and moral irresponsibility is the quality of leadership afforded the people. While this does not excuse the faults into which the people may fall, it does suggest the crucial importance of quality leadership. No group is likely to rise higher than the level of its leadership. Hence, "My contention is with you, O priest" (v. 4). Basically, there are five areas of guilt characteristic of religious leadership.

First, religious leaders may have no personal relationship with the Lord: the priests "have rejected knowledge" (v. 6). Perfunctory service born of a superficial professionalism soon abandons dynamic, relational-oriented experiences with the Lord. Appropriately, the people of Israel were destroyed not for a lack of "things" but for a "lack of knowledge"—with the obvious implication that this "knowledge" relates to the Lord.

Second, religious leaders forget the Lord: the priests have "forgotten the law of your God" (v. 6). To "forget" in the Old Testament

means more than a lapse of memory. Just as "hear" often means
to obey, so remember often means more than merely to call to mind.
Forgetting means more than mere forgetfulness. For example, "Take
heed . . . lest you *forget* the covenant of the LORD your God . . .
and make a graven image" (Deut. 4:23). Also, to say that the Lord
"will not fail you or destroy you or *forget* the covenant" (Deut.
4:31) means more than that the Lord will no longer be able to call
the covenant to mind. It means that his actions will be grounded
in the covenant relationship. To forget the covenant connotes a
quality of apostasy.

Third, the enormity of the priests' sin is graphically portrayed
in the suggestion that their sin was in direct proportion to their
number! "The more they increased, the more they sinned against
me" (v. 7). The word "sin" is the common one, suggesting "to miss
the mark." The direct translation of the phrase is graphic: "According
to their multiplication they sinned against me." Sin separates religious
leaders from God. They, too, "miss the mark" established for them
by the covenant relationship.

Fourth, religious leaders may become exploitive of worshipers.
There was an eagerness that the people sin (v. 8). In a religious
system such as Israel's in which religious leaders received their
livelihood from portions of sacrificial offerings, whether animal or
cereal, such a temptation is all the more real. Such a temptation
to exploit the religious needs of persons seeking God is constant
and unchanging, as much a temptation now as then. Wolff translates
this phrase in v. 8: "They yearn for them with greedy throats."
Contemporary charlatans who exploit the religious needs of other
persons are as immoral and as responsible for the demise of dynamic
religious experience as ever were the corrupt priests of Hosea's day.

Fifth, religious leaders have "forsaken the Lord to cherish harlotry"
(RSV, v. 10). Of this verse Wolff says, "For the first time in the
prophetic writings—and in the general history of religion, for that
matter—the concept 'apostasy' appears." [1] However one may deal
with apostasy from the broader theological perspective or from the

---

[1] Hans Walter Wolff, *Hosea,* "Hermeneia: A Critical and Historical Commentary
on the Bible" (Philadelphia: Fortress Press, 1974), p. 82.

position of the New Testament, Hosea assumes that the priests of his day had forsaken the Lord. Whatever explanation one may offer, persons continue to abandon the Lord to serve other affections and loyalties which have supplanted the priority the Lord once held.

2. Responsibility and Guilt of the People, 4:11-14

There are four areas in which the people at large are guilty before the "court" which the Lord holds.

First, the people are guilty of a general lack of discernment, characterized by the indictment "wine and new wine take away the understanding" (v. 11). As Hosea suggested previously, "My people are destroyed for a lack of knowledge" (v. 6). As alcohol can dull and finally stupefy one's powers of reason and control, so individuals may lose their spiritual understanding. Only a stupefied, senseless people abandon the Lord. But they will.

Second, the people had abandoned the Lord and the established media of revelation (v. 12). They had turned aside from the revelation of God to revelation perceived through their objects of divination—"a thing of wood," "their staff." Rather than turning to the word of the prophet for an oracle, they turned to their idolatrous objects. Their second error was the abandonment of normative revelation.

Third, religious compromise characterized the religious experience of the people (vv. 12b-13). A "spirit of harlotry has led them astray." That is, an irrational power leads men to forsake the Lord. Later, Hosea returns to the same theme (5:4). There is something demonic in the irrational manner in which the positive concern of a person for God can be led astray by alien powers.

Fourth, immorality characterized both men and women (v. 14). Sexual union with a "sacred prostitute" ("sacred" only in the sense that she was dedicated to the god) was one aspect of Baalism, fertility being a fundamental aspect of that religion. In words open to no reason for misunderstanding, Hosea characterized the men as having sexual relations with both common harlots and cult prostitutes associated with their compromised worship. Also, daughters "play the harlot" and "your brides . . . commit adultery" (v. 14). Seldom does one find a more depressing portrait of depraved life than this

father-daughter-wife scene in which all are involved in immoral
sexual behavior.

III. Results of Immoral and Apostate Conduct, 4:4-14

Intertwined with the description of offenses by both priests and
people are descriptions of the specific results of such actions. In
almost every instance, punishment is inherent within the deed.

1. Judgment Is Indiscriminate, v. 8

"It shall be like people, like priest" (v. 9); suggests that the priests
are not exempt from judgment. Some may have concluded that
although the populace was accountable and, therefore, subject to
judgment, the special position of the priests brought some type of
impunity. This is not the case. As then so today—it shall be like
people, like religious leader. God does not discriminate.

2. Judgment Is Specific, vv. 5-14

Judgment is not defined in vague, abstract terms. Rather, Hosea
describes specific results of specific actions for specific groups of
persons: to each his own.

First, there are inevitable consequences for religious leaders guilty
of apostasy and morally irresponsible conduct. Hosea suggests the
eventual dissolution of both priest and nation (vv. 5-6). Both prophet
and priest "shall stumble," and "your mother" (Israel, most probably)
will be destroyed. Also, religious leaders who reject experiential
knowledge of God are themselves "rejected" (v. 6). Those who forget
the Lord will find that their children will be forgotten; an especially
awesome threat in the context of an hereditary priesthood.

The priesthood was a glorious position in Israel. Even their clothing
suggested glory and beauty: "holy garments for Aaron your brother,
for glory and beauty" (Ex. 28:2). But priests, or twentieth-century
religious leaders, will find their glory turned to shame (v. 7) because
of their faithlessness.

Coupled with these consequences for religious leaders, is a thoroughgoing sense of dissatisfaction and frustration: "They shall eat,
but not be satisfied" (v. 10; cf. Isa. 55:1 ff). The phrase "play the
harlot, but not multiply" suggests that although they may participate
in fertility rites associated with Baalism, there will be no multiplica-

tion of flock or field because of this. The phrase hardly refers to offspring of other forms of prostitution from which children are not desired. In effect, you may abandon the Lord for spurious forms of religious experience but it will be to no fruitful avail.

Second, specific consequences of the people's sins are also isolated. In the summation of his case against the people, Hosea affirms "Therefore . . ." (vv. 13-14). Both immorality in the family and the disintegration of the nation are associated with the apostasy of the people. It shall be like father, like daughter and wives. Men who cohabit with prostitutes can hardly expect of their daughters or wives a higher standard than they themselves demonstrate. In a way unique for Old Testament times, Hosea stressed the fact that there is no double standard: one for men and another for women. Both are held accountable to the same norm; a fact which is all the more important because of the generally secondary role of woman in the Old Testament. How graphic and relevant is Hosea's final observation: "A people without understanding shall come to ruin" (v. 14). When people have no understanding of the Lord, no "knowledge of God," ruin is their inevitable companion.

IV. Reproach to Judah Based on Israel's Experience, 4:15-19

In a warning which probably dates to the time when the book of Hosea had passed into Judah following the fall of the Northern Kingdom, a disciple of the prophet appended a warning to Judah. Or, as some suggest, Hosea himself may have turned aside from addressing Israel to caution the Southern Kingdom.

The prophet affirms that we should learn from others. Why does every generation have to learn for itself that which could have been learned from history? Whether it is one's own children or a nation, both seem determined to learn by hard experience what could have been learned from the hard experiences of others! In this regard, Hosea poses three warnings—still appropriate.

First, do not become like apostate and immoral people. "Let not Judah become guilty"—whatever Israel may have done (v. 15). Do not become like others by imitating their compromised worship. He warns Judah about entering religious centers associated with apostate religious practices; even calling Bethel (house of God) "Beth-aven" (house of iniquity, or nothingness). Not only do not imitate their worship, but do not follow their example of obedience (v. 16). Anyone who may have had anything to do with a stubborn calf, or other animal, can appreciate Hosea's analogy: "Like a stubborn heifer, Israel is stubborn" (v. 16). Can you deal with such a stubborn animal as gently as you would with a lamb? Hardly! (v. 16).

Second, a good way to avoid apostasy and immorality is to leave those alone who are involved in such activities (vv. 17-18). "Ephraim is joined to idols, let him alone" (v. 17). Israel's idolatry is adequate cause to leave them alone. While the prophet should hardly be quoted in support of a superficial self-righteousness which stands with superiority over persons, the prophet does counsel a course of noninvolvement with religious and moral apostates. One response to evil of any time is to flee from it. Not only should Judah leave Israel alone because of her idolatry; Israel is "a band of drunkards, they give themselves to harlotry" (v. 18). People who "love shame more than their glory" (v. 18) are best avoided. So, on both religious and generally moral grounds Judah is advised to leave Israel alone.

Third, believers should learn from the fate of others (v. 19). Destruction and shame have swept over Israel, "a wind has wrapped them in its wings." What destroys one nation or individual can destroy another. Now that it is too late, Israel is "ashamed because of their altars" (v. 19). Shame when it comes prior to judgment can lead to renewal that effects new life and hope. But shame after the fact of judgment leads only to regret. Hosea's advice remains sound: seeing the destruction and shame wrought by apostasy and immorality, avoid such a way of life. Why insist upon experiencing in your own existence what you can learn from observing the existence of others?

3

When God Withdraws

5:1-14

Is it possible to seek God, yet fail to find him? Hosea affirms that however frequently we seek to find God, however multitudinous our efforts, we do not automatically find him: "With their flocks and herds they shall go to seek the LORD, but they will not find him; he has withdrawn from them" (5:6). Attitude is of primary consideration. One should recognize that "finding the Lord" depends upon the manner in which we seek him: ". . . you will seek the LORD your God, and you will find him, *if you search after him with all your heart and with all your soul*" (Deut. 4:29, italics added).

The withdrawal of God is a reality which should be taken with due seriousness. Helmut Thielicke once wrote of "the silence of God" in a book by the same title; examining those dismaying times when one experiences the awesome silence of God. What precipitates this "withdrawal of God"—assuming that the silence of God is a reality associated with religious experience?

I. Condemnation of Religious Leadership, 5:1-2

Hosea returns to the causative role of religious leaders in the disintegration of covenant relationships. Ineffective leadership may not excuse the failures of the people. It does clarify one reason for the erosion of religious commitment and the emergence of faithlessness. Hosea identifies the *participants* (v. 1), isolates their *practices* (v. 2), and clarifies their *punishment* (v. 2).

First, religious leaders are uniquely responsible for the quality of justice in a land. Three ranges of leadership are involved. Hosea addresses the priests, "Hear this, O priests!" But he moves beyond them to the "house of Israel," referring in all probability to clan chieftains. He also includes the "house of the king"—the princes

31

or others who comprised the king's court. In each instance, the summons to hear is progressively more intense: "hear this . . . give heed . . . hearken."

Rather than interpreting "judgment" (v. 1) as punishment it is more probable that one should interpret the word as "justice." Each group—priests, clan chieftains, and court officials—has a unique responsibility. They are accountable for justice.

The relationship between religious leaders specified by Hosea and the maintenance of justice is clear. It was the priests' responsibility to discern and proclaim divine law. The clan chieftain was especially responsible for the local administration of justice, probably at the city gates. The royal court probably refers to those gathered around the king; although not a "court" as we think of it today.

Second, rather than promoting justice in the land, religious leaders trapped the people (v. 2). Using a series of metaphors taken from the hunter's equipment, Hosea suggests that leaders responsible for justice had been a "snare," a "net," and a "pit" for the people. A polarization of function had occurred on the part of national leadership. Although responsible for justice, leaders had acted with injustice. Those events of injustice, figuratively speaking, had occurred at sites uniquely associated with apostasy: Mizpah, Tabor, and Shittim. Israel had, in essence, returned to former ways of irresponsibility.

The statement that the Lord will "chastise all of them" is best interpreted from the positive perspective of discipline. "Chastise" has overtones of teaching which are significant. The root word is associated with instruction in the family (Deut. 8:5; 21:18; Prov. 4:1) and particularly a father's instruction of his son (Prov. 31:1; Deut. 8:5).

II. Context for National Apostasy, 5:3-7

What attitudes characterize people in their departure from the Lord? Hosea isolates at least five basic areas of conduct which were related to Israel's separation from the Lord.

First, infidelity such as that between Gomer and Hosea separates (v. 3). The prophet is the subject of the address in verse 3; although at first examination, it might appear that God is the speaker. Since God is object in verse 4*a* and the Lord is object in verse 4*b*, it appears legitimate to assume that the speaker in verse 3 is the prophet. The verse is a "messenger speech," however, and the prophet is spokesman for the Lord. To this extent, therefore, it is the Lord who speaks.

The grammatical structure of verse 3 underscores the fact that the Lord knows without question the true character of individual and nation. One might translate the phrase "I, on my part, I know Ephraim" (v. 3). There is no place to hide one's sin from the searching scrutiny of God: "Israel is not hid from me." Because Israel has "played the harlot," she has become defiled, reflecting the common idea of uncleanness associated with improper sexual relationships (cf. Lev. 18:20). Defilement also may suggest the cultic nature of Israel's sin as well, implying that participation in the false worship of Baal resulted in ritual defilement. But the primary intention is to suggest that infidelity is a form of prostitution which alienates one from God.

Second, return for such people is no longer a human possibility; return in such a context demands divine action (v. 4). In what might well be termed an "argumentative speech" or "disputation," Hosea argues that the return of Israel is no longer humanly possible for at least two reasons: (1) *"Their deeds do not permit them to return."* Individuals and nations continue to become so involved with actions which are contrary to the will of God that their deeds bind them. Their deeds will not permit them to return to the Lord. Loving what they are doing more than they love the Lord, they choose to continue with sinful pleasures rather than return to the Lord and his often stringent demands. (2) Also, a *"spirit of harlotry is within them"* (that is, the nation). As in 4:12, so here, Hosea ascribes Israel's irrational rejection of the Lord to a spirit of harlotry; an internal disposition set against the Lord. We do well to ask ourselves, "What is the dynamic, energizing power of my life—the reality of God's spirit, or an alien spirit hostile to the purposes of God?"

Third, pride precludes a return to the Lord: "The pride of Israel testifies to his face" (v. 5). Whether intellectual pride, moral pride,

or spiritual pride, the effect is the same. Seeking to be more than
"man," persons seek to be as God (Gen. 3:5). As Niebuhr once
suggested, we deny the "image of God" in at least two ways. Through
pride we seek to become more than "man," while through debauchery
we are content to live as less than "man," living on the animal
level of existence.

Fourth, superficial worship does not guarantee the presence of
God (v. 6). Formal worship of the eighth century B.C. in Israel was
"prosperous." People thronged the shrines and there is every evidence
from prophets such as Amos, Hosea, Isaiah, and Micah to suggest
that externally religion was popular (cf. Amos 4:4 ff; 5:21 ff; Isa.
1:10 ff; Mic. 6:6 ff).

"Flocks and herds" suggest the multiplicity of Israel's offerings.
Despite the number of man's external acts of worship, God withdraws
in the presence of hypocrisy and the prostitution of one's religious
commitment (v. 3), the entanglement of one's life with deeds that
do not permit one to return (v. 4), as well as an element of pride
which leads a nation "to stumble" (v. 5). Then as now, "the Lord
has withdrawn from them—they will not find him." One may seek
and not find; just as one may seek and find. The determinative
qualities are internal not external. As Micah assessed the issue in
his own day, the Lord is not impressed by "thousands of rams . . .
ten thousands of rivers of oil"—not even with the possible sacrifice
of one's own child (Mic. 6:7). Rather, "What does the LORD require
of you but to do justice, and to love kindness, and to walk humbly
with your God?" (Mic. 6:8). It is this quality of dedication which
is prerequisite to genuine meeting with the Lord.

Fifth, people who deal "faithlessly" with the Lord awake to find
themselves alienated, estranged, separated from the Lord (v. 7). In
a phrase reminiscent of the Gomer experience, Hosea indicates that
the people have dealt "faithlessly" with the Lord (v. 7). The word
translated "faithlessly" means to act or deal treacherously. Compare
Isaiah 24:16 for striking alliteration: "For the treacherous deal
treacherously, the treacherous deal very treacherously." Most persons distinguish between "crime" and "treason." Abandonment of the
Lord is "treason" not a "crime." It is an act of treachery. The repudi-

ation . of covenant bonds is akin to the rejection of national
loyalty, as in a case of treason. Israel's action, or our own, was
treasonable to the extent that it represented a basic betrayal of
loyalty and commitment.

III. Consequences of Rejecting the Lord, 5:8-14

Three consequences emerge from the rejection of the Lord: historical manifestation of judgment through civil war (vv. 8 ff; cf. 5:8
to 6:6), false reliance upon international alliances (v. 13), and the
chastening presence of God in history (vv. 14 ff).

First, the certainty of judgment in history is affirmed by the
prophet: "I declare what is sure" (vv. 8-12). The Syro-Ephraimitic
war (734-733 B.C.) was a time of civil war between Judah on the
one hand and Israel-Syria on the other. It was a time of what Wolff
called "brotherwar" (*bruderkreig*). Danger approaches Israel from
the direction of Jerusalem, as indicated by the geographical location
of successive cities mentioned in verse 8. Judah's move to the north
is preparation for Israel's "desolation," her "day of punishment"
(v. 9). History is the arena for God's action, whether in grace or
judgment. One continuing responsibility of a "prophetic community," the church, is to interpret history in the light of God, his
will and his purposes.

Judah's violation of Israel's border is likened to the action of "those
who remove the landmark"; a reprehensible deed in ancient Israel
(cf. Deut. 19:14; 27:17). But Hosea also turns again to Israel and
suggests that he had been "crushed in judgment"; the Lord had
become as destructive for Israel as a moth was to fabric (v. 12).
Hosea was concerned about the *degeneration* of leadership (v. 10),
the *destruction* of the nation (v. 11), and the *disintegration* of Israel
and Judah. The silent but certain effects of God's judgment are
appropriately likened to both moth and dry rot (v. 12).

Second, although the pressure of circumstances drove Israel and
Judah to see their need, they sought to alleviate that need through
political alliance rather than through reliance upon the Lord (v. 13).
While such a passage should not be taken to mean that nations
should make no alliances in contemporary world politics, it does

suggest that *the internal character of a nation is of greater ultimate significance for its survival than are its external alliances.* More specifically, both Israel and Judah had paid tribute to Tiglath-Pileser III of Assyria. Hosea is referred to on a stone tablet inscription of Tiglath-Pileser III as having paid tribute, and a few months before the same thing was done by Ahaz in Judah (cf. Isa. 7:1 ff; 2 Kings 16:7 ff). The implications are obvious: national character is more likely to produce stability than a foreign policy which flits from one nation to another seeking international support (cf. Hos. 7:11).

Third, the Lord is identified as one who stands beyond history, though acting within history. He uses the events of history in such providential fashion as to chasten his people (v. 14). He is described as a lion who pounces upon his victim (cf. Amos 1:2; 3:8) and then carries the prey off to his lair where no one shall be able to rescue. Whether the passage refers specifically to exile cannot be determined. But it does convey the concept of exile. The purpose of such action is redemptive and not merely punitive.

The "withdrawal of God" is not designed as a permanent forfeiture of divine presence. To the contrary, the withdrawal of God is designed to lead men to see their need for him. As often suggested, we seldom appreciate anything fully until we lose it. The Lord will "return again to my place, *until* they acknowledge their guilt and seek my face" (v. 15). Exposed to the silence of God, men long for the voice of God. Devoid of the presence of God, persons desire the reality of God. Abandoned to the ravages of history, men long for the grace and forgiveness of God.

4

God in Perplexity

6:1-11

If understood literally, the phrase "God in perplexity" may suggest a contradiction in the nature and character of God. But here the word is used figuratively, not literally. It is an altogether anthropomorphic expression, speaking of God in human terminology. In what other language may we speak of God than in the language of our common humanity, utilizing various figures of speech to portray aspects of God as we experience him?

The intent of chapter 6 is obvious. Man's vacillation in first repenting and then turning again to his sin is beyond comprehension. One may hear to this day parental exasperation expressed in a variety of ways. For example, "I don't know what I am going to do. . . ." Hosea's picture of the Lord is much like that. Surveying the character of Israel's repentance, coupled with the transient nature of her steadfast love, the prophet shares the divine exasperation with his people: "What shall I do with you, O Ephraim? What shall I do with you, O Judah?" (v. 4). Has the situation greatly changed? Does the Lord still experience the same anxious exasperation? Is he "in perplexity" concerning what can be done with a people whose devotion is so fleeting, whose repentance is so superficial?

The message of Hosea 6:1-11 focuses upon three themes: the withdrawal of God and the confession of man (6:1-3; cf. 5:15), the perplexity of God and the action of man (6:4-10), and a warning to Judah (6:11).

I. The Withdrawal of God and the Confession of Man, 6:1-3

Hosea 6:1-6 constitutes a lamentation of repentance (cf. 6:1-3) closely followed by the Lord's response (6:4 ff). The passage suggests that the withdrawal of God (5:15) leads to man's repentance (6:1-3), however short lived that repentance may be (6:4 ff).

First the withdrawal of God is designed to lead one to repentance and renewal (5:15). There is some question whether verse 15 serves as the conclusion of chapter 5 or as the opening premise of chapter 6. A pattern of long standing suggests that it be taken as the opening verse for chapter 6 (cf. RSV). Technically, the verse should probably be taken as the concluding verse to chapter 5 (cf. NEB). In any event, the concept of the withdrawal of God serves as the backdrop for the lamentation of repentance in 6:1-3.

In addition to Hosea's emphasis on the withdrawal of God, Amos also envisioned such a time: a time when ". . . they shall run to and fro, to seek the word of the LORD, but they shall not find it" (Amos 8:12). This kind of withdrawal is neither absolute nor is it irrevocable. Rather than punitive, the intention of the action is positive. Perhaps through the temporary loss of God, which may seem permanent at the time and in fact apart from repentance and renewal may be permanent, individuals may be lead to repentance and renewal of life. Note, for example, the qualifying *"until"* (v. 15).

Second, an appropriate state of repentance assumes a *return* to the Lord: "Come, let us *return* to the LORD . . ." (v. 1). Quite significantly, the verb translated "return" is a most common word for repentance in the Old Testament (*shuv,* turn, turn back, return). For illustrations of the word as a specific symbol of repentance, one might examine passages such as Hosea 11:5; Isaiah 6:10; 10:22; Jeremiah 3:7,12; 4:1; 5:3. To "repent" is to turn around, return to the Lord. Such repentance is grounded in the sure conviction that those who have been torn may be healed; those who have been stricken may be bound up. The phrase "that he may heal" is easily misunderstood to mean that the Lord has torn *so* that he may heal. Translated more directly, the passage states, "He, he has torn and he will heal us." As NEB translates: "For he has torn us and will heal us, he has struck us and he will bind up our wounds" (v. 1). This is the action of a loving, redeeming God who comes to chasten his people. He does smite. But he also heals. Judgment is never God's last word. Curative, healing grace always follows judgment.

Third, an appropriate state of repentance leads to *renewal* of life (v. 2). The "third day" had unique significance in Israel, as did the use of the number three in other contexts—as in the case of a three-day journey or preparation to meet the Lord on the third day at Sinai (Ex. 19:1 ff). In this instance, raising up the nation to live before the Lord occurs on the third day. Two verbs convey the action of the verse: "he will make us *live*" (RSV, revive) and "he will *raise us up.*" The effect of national resurrection is life lived "to the LORD": "And in his presence we may live" (NEB).

Fourth, repentance should lead to unique *knowledge* of the Lord (v. 3): "Let us know, let us press on to know the LORD." To "know the LORD" suggests personal, experiential knowledge. Such personal relationship with the Lord is the ultimate objective of repentance. Renewal of life leads to a closer relationship to him who is the source of life.

The certainty of such knowledge is suggested in the prophet's statement that "his going forth is sure as the dawn." While there are positive connotations associated with this element of certainty, there is also the possibility of a presumptive attitude. The lamentation of repentance is exceedingly wholesome when taken at face value. But it is equally superficial when viewed from the perspective of a possibly hypocritical stance. One can easily presume upon the grace of God by assuming that the coming of God is automatic, the assured, guaranteed response of the Lord to man's confession. In this particular instance, the following verse (v. 4) suggests that Israel's response in repentance was essentially superficial. It was certainly transient, as fleeting as the morning cloud or the dew that passes so quickly with the first heat of day. It is natural to question the viability of a repentance so transient as this. Hypocritical phrases of repentance are of no avail. Renewal comes only when the heart is rightly related to the Lord: "A broken and contrite heart, O God, thou wilt not despise" (Ps. 51:17).

II. The Perplexity of God and the Action of Man, 6:4-10

Throughout the remainder of the chapter, the primary focus is upon God's amazement at the quality of Israel's fidelity (v. 4) and the consequences of infidelity for the people of God (vv. 5-7). As though to thwart any objection to his indictment, Hosea cites specific conduct at various centers such as Gilead and Shechem which validate the accusation of infidelity (vv. 8-10).

1. God's Amazement, 6:4-6

The questions which appear in verse 4 are clearly anthropomorphic; God is spoken of in human terms. As men are amazed and perplexed at the irrational, incomprehensible action of some persons, so the Lord is amazed at the brevity of Israel's fidelity. But more than this, what is God to do with people who so trifle with great issues such as repentance (vv. 1-3) and whose loyalty is so brief? The pertinence of the issue may be intensified if contemporary persons substitute the name of their own nation or even their personal names for Ephraim and Judah. Why not substitute one's own name: "What shall I do with you _____? What shall I do with you, _____?" (v. 4).

The basis for the Lord's continuing concern is apparent: "Your love is like a morning cloud, like the dew that goes early away" (v. 4). "Love" means steadfast love, fidelity, loyal love—that quality of love within covenant relationship which prompts loyalty. For Israel, this quality was like ground fog that vanishes with the appearance of the morning sun. It was like the dew that so quickly dissipates before the warmth of the sun's rays. How vivid is the prophet's characterization of the transient, fleeting nature of those qualities of devotion often expressed toward the Lord!

What precipitates this charge of transient loyalty? *First,* the prophet may have in mind those qualities of vacillation which are perennial accompaniments of religious commitment. For this is a continuing issue for serious-minded persons. Commitment does waver. Loyalty does weaken. *Second,* although the lamentation of repentance is outwardly a vivid description of that quality of repentance which characterizes a dynamic relationship with the Lord (vv. 1-3), it is possible that the passage, especially the closing verse (v. 3) has about it an almost presumptive note. One may be sure of the Lord's response to genuine repentance—unquestionably so. But there is also a flippant, superficial attitude which looks upon repentance as a license to sin, assured that man has only to repent for God to forgive. This is a constant hazard to experiencing genuine repentance. *Third,* is it not possible that within verses 1-3 there are interwoven aspects of Baalism which suggest that the lamentation of repentance is not the firm affirmation of loyalty to the Lord that the passage may suggest upon first reading? The dying-rising pattern (v. 2), as well as the association of the Lord's presence with the dawn, the showers, and the spring rains may suggest aspects of nature religion. In any event, the lamentation of repentance in verses 1-3 failed to evoke qualities of life consistent with the affirmation of repentance. The crucial test for measuring the validity of an experience of repentance is not so much the nature of the confession but the quality of life evoked by the experience. In the case of Israel, repentance failed to evoke the steadfast love which is essential to dynamic covenant life.

The consequences of Israel's infidelity are clear: "I have hewn them by the prophets" (v. 5). Hosea probably had in mind those earlier prophets of Israel, such as Elijah, Ahijah, Micaiah ben Imlah—prophets whose words were a sword.

The "word of the LORD" is dynamic and powerful; an instrument in the prophets' arsenal. For Jeremiah, the Lord's word was like a hammer, breaking the rock in pieces; like a flail, separating wheat and chaff; like a consuming fire, destroying the chaff (Jer. 23:28 ff). The "word of the LORD" carries within itself the power of its own fulfillment: "It shall not return to me empty, but it shall accomplish that which I purpose, and prosper in the thing for which I sent it" (Isa. 55:11). Prophets, whether ancient or modern, need only proclaim that "word" faithfully; then await the fulfillment of that word.

That the Lord is more concerned with character and dynamic relationships within the covenant than he is with formal structures of religion is clearly reflected in Hosea's statement: "For I desire steadfast love and not sacrifice, the knowledge of God, rather than burnt offerings" (v. 6). "Steadfast love" is a translation of the same word translated "love" (v. 4) and "kindness" (4:1). More than superficial forms of worship such as "sacrifice" and "burnt offering," the

Lord wants a love that is steadfast, coupled with a knowledge of himself that pervades the whole of an individual's life. This is not to say that Hosea or other prophets were intrinsically opposed to the concept of worship. Rather, they opposed abuses in worship, worship as it had developed in their time. Quite significantly, no prophet ever offered an alternate to replace public worship. Rather, they called for the reformation of worship. Yet some went even beyond this. They emphasized that more fundamental than formally structured worship is one's dynamic relationship with the Lord.

One's personal experience with the Lord stands in higher priority than any form of ritual or public worship, as in the later suggestion by Jeremiah. He observed that Israel had a dynamic experience with the Lord in the Exodus event prior to the giving of instructions concerning worship (cf. Jer. 7:21 ff). The importance of the priority of experience over formalized worship appears in the statement of Jesus when he was condemned for permitting disciples to pluck grain on the sabbath: "I tell you, something greater than the temple is here. And if you had known what this means, 'I desire mercy, and not sacrifice,' you would not have condemned the guiltless. For the Son of man is lord of the sabbath" (Matt. 12:6 ff). Hosea and Jesus are at one in affirming that in one's personal, living experience with God "something greater than the temple is here."

2. Man's Action, 6:7-10

The catalog of sins in verses 7-10 clearly are directed against priests guilty of violating covenant relationships, whether these relate to civil, political, or religious crimes. Are the actions described here to be taken literally, or are they means of describing the heinous conduct of the priests? Did priests actually lie in wait for people? Did they murder on the way to Shechem (which was a city of refuge)? Or is this a way of describing figuratively their reprehensible actions? One should not be dogmatic at this juncture. Suffice it to say that the action of the priests is used as a means of illustrating covenant infidelity.

There is equal uncertainty concerning the specific sites mentioned by Hosea: Adam, Gilead, Shechem, Bethel (or, "the house of Israel," v. 10). The Hebrew text reads "like Adam" in verse 7, but there is an almost universal interpretation in contemporary commentaries which emends this to "at" and assumes that "Adam" refers to a site at the mouth of the Jabbok river (probably modern Tell el-Damje). The meaning of the text is not dependent upon knowing precisely what occurred at each of these sites. The point of the prophet is simple but important. In contemporary actions the people, epitomized in the priests and perhaps acting in concert with them, acted in such manner as to reflect infidelity to the covenant. Hosea's intention is clear. Man's action validates God's amazement. What *can* God do with a people who affirm repentance (vv. 1-3) but act in such fashion (vv. 7-10) as to reveal a basic infidelity to covenant relationships (vv. 4-7)?

III. A Warning from History, 6:11

Verse 11 is a warning to Judah based upon the experience of Israel: "For you also, O Judah, a harvest is appointed" (v. 11). The warning was probably added to the text by an inspired and insightful scribe at a time when the sayings of Hosea had passed to the Southern Kingdom after the fall of Samaria. Some do, however, assume that Hosea turns to Judah to warn her in light of Israel's failure. The warning is grounded in history and suggests that the people of God should be able to learn from the discipline of history. There is an inevitable fate awaiting those whose superficial views toward repentance lead not only to unfaithful relationships but to eventual national destruction.

5

Half-Baked Religion

7:1-16

The expression "half-baked" is as old as Hosea and is as current as contemporary actions reflected through daily news media. The word has long since lost its literal meaning and has come to be applied to attitudes or actions which are in some way lacking. Described as "a cake not turned" (v. 8), Israel was guilty of duplicity in wide ranges of her relationships. As a cake of bread cooked on a baking stone—done on one side but raw on the other—Israel was well described as "half-baked." A thoroughgoing duplicity characterized her morality, integrity, responsibility, and spirituality. She was corrupt (vv. 1-7), compromised (vv. 8-10), capricious (vv. 11-13), and careless (vv. 14-16).

I. Half-baked Morality: A Corrupt Community, 7:1-7

The corruption of Israel was manifest in both social and political actions. Her actions precluded restoration and healing with which the Lord would have healed the land (cf. 6:1; 7:1). The situation was apparently both hopeless (vv. 1-2) and complex (vv. 3-7).

1. The hopelessness of the human situation, 7:1-2

First, the attitude of God suggests that grace transcends judgment, but that man's sin may preclude forgiveness (v. 1). Restoration, not renunciation, is the purpose of God for his people. He desires to "restore the fortunes of my people" (6:11). But at the very moment that he would heal Israel the continuing corruption of the land is revealed (vv. 1-2). Moral corruption not only denies the validity of one's stated repentance, it thwarts God's grace and forgiveness.

Second, specific actions make restoration impossible (vv. 1-2). Israel's character was unstable, their deeds insincere, their lawlessness indicted by God, and their concept of God insufficient (vv. 1-2).

44

Such corruption of the nation (Ephraim) was confirmed by the "wicked deeds of Samaria," the capital city. Specifically, "they deal falsely, the thief breaks in, and the bandits raid without" (v. 1). That action was grossly inconsistent with Israel's earlier confession of repentance (6:1-3) but equally consistent with Hosea's insistence that their steadfast love was "like a morning cloud, like the dew that goes early away" (6:4). What *can* God do (6:4)—when every time he is at the point of restoring the people, renewed evidences of continued corruption are uncovered?

Those who have entered into relationship with the Lord forget too soon that he not only knows but remembers immoral action. God is not only aware, he is committed to bring offenders to accountability: "They do not consider that I remember all their evil works" (v. 2). There is a self-destructive, suicidal dynamic associated with immoral action. Deeds of the quality described by Hosea "encompass" the people (7:2). Not only do one's deeds so imprison one's life that they prevent an appropriate return to the Lord (cf. 5:4), they bring with them their own awesome judgment. We do reap what we sow, and more. Yet this is more than an automatic process within the moral order of the universe. Retribution occurs "before my face." That is, the Lord is uniquely related to retributive judgment attendant to immoral action. There is a personal relationship involved in judgment just as there is a personal relationship involved in redemption. Both occur "before the LORD's face."

2. The Complexity of the Situation, 7:3-7

A full range of social and political elements in Israel was involved in the "half-baked morality" which Hosea described: king, princes, and people. The problem was universal, embracing every facet of society. The "wickedness" which Hosea describes as having made "the king glad" (v. 3) was most likely associated with the period of violent revolutions in Israel during the mid-eighth century B.C. The king who assumed the throne following such a period of violent revolution was well described as "glad" (v. 3).

The deception which characterized people associated with the overthrow of the former king was appropriately described as adultery: "They are all adulterers" (v. 4). Throughout verses 4-7 the plural pronoun (they, their, them) apparently refers to the people. They are likened to a heated oven—smoldering while the baker was at work kneading the bread, but stirred to burning heat during the time the bread was fermenting (v. 4). On the day of coronation, the princes became sick with wine and the king stretched out his hand "with mockers"—a vivid picture of degradation within the royal court (v. 5). The hearts of the people burn with "intrigue," "their anger smolders" (v. 6). Compared to heated ovens, the people devour their rulers (v. 7), and as a consequence of the chaotic rebellions of that era, "all their kings have fallen" (v. 7). Despite this lack of leadership, "none of them calls upon me" (v. 7).

Is there any surprise that, given the complexity of the situation in the mid-eighth century B.C., the Lord could not restore his people (6:11)? Whether in the action of people who deal falsely in a land where thieves and bandits were prominent (v. 1), or in the action of people who acted in revolution to replace kings, there were adequate evidences to conclude that the community was corrupt. Israel's morality was "half-baked"—less than it should have been, by far.

II. Half-baked Integrity: A Compromised Community, 7:8-10

Integrity suggests "wholeness" and those qualities associated with loyalty and commitment. Hosea was convinced that the community of faith, Israel, had so compromised itself that they had suffered major reversals in their religious commitment, their national strength, and their religious experience with the Lord.

Compromise is suggested in the premise that Ephraim (which is used synonymously with Israel in Hosea) "mixes himself with the peoples; Ephraim is a cake not turned" (v. 8). Like a pancake that is done on one side but raw on the other, so Israel was compromised in each of several areas of her experiences.

First, compromise had lead Israel to blend her religious experience with the culture of the era (v. 8). The phrase "mixes himself with the peoples" refers to the way in which the worship of the Lord had been compromised with elements of Baalism (cf. 2:6 ff; 16 ff; 4:12 ff). The phrase may refer on the other hand, to international

political alliances. Throughout the history of Israel, primary emphasis
was placed upon complete fidelity to the LORD. Israel was to be
a "separate people, dedicated wholly to the LORD." Prophets and
other writers constantly warned against the danger of diluting faith
in the Lord through marriage with non-Israelites; a warning which
had theological rather than sociological foundations. Despite the
obvious fact that we are all caught up in the world together, the
people of God are to be a distinctive people. As Jesus later was
to suggest, they are to be in the world, but not of the world—par-
ticipating fully in the world, but not belonging to the world (John
15:18 ff; 17:15 ff). How far had Israel fallen from that ideal, mixing
himself among the peoples, a half-baked cake!

  Second, compromise saps the strength, leaving one unaware of
the loss of strength (v. 9). Reference to "aliens" who "devour his
strength" refers to political compromise which lead Israelite kings
to pay tribute to a major nation such as Assyria or to enter into
a league with Syria against Judah (733). In other ways, also, Israel
succumbed to the rising power of Assyria in the latter half of the
eighth century B.C.

  A note of tragedy rests in the fact that "he knows it not." There
are fewer more pathetic situations than one in which an individual
loses power and influence without being aware of it himself. Consequently, he becomes a joke or a buffoon at best, a fool at worst.
The "gray hairs," which signify advancing age and a comparable
lessening of vital power are sprinkled upon him, and "he knows
it not" (v. 9). Israel was finished. Everyone knew it before Israel.
This is the way of compromise. It saps your strength without your
awareness, until suddenly you are no more than a joke among those
who see you as you actually are, a buffoon or a fool who cannot
see what compromise has done.

  Third, compromise separates from God (v. 10). Wolff says that
the phrase "a cake not turned" (v. 8) suggests that although it is
time for Israel to turn to the Lord, he has not done so. While this
is attractive it is not conclusive. Verse 10 does however affirm that
despite motivating experiences which should have lead Israel to
return they have not turned. Price precludes penitence and restoration.

Pride

Hosea implies that, as suggested previously (5:5), it is the pride of Israel which precludes return: "The pride of Israel witnesses against him" (v. 10). When pride is placed on the witness stand its nature argues for return. The negative results of Israel's pride were adequate grounds for motivating a return to the Lord. Despite this, however, "They do not return to the LORD their God, nor seek him, for all this" (v. 10). Compromise in the area of national politics, which was never distinct from theological issues in the Old Testament, separated Israel from the Lord. Compromise has not changed in its basic effect. It still separates people from God.

III. Half-baked Responsibility: A Capricious Community, 7:11-13

In the context of national and international responsibilities, Israel demonstrated an almost total irresponsibility: half-baked in the sense that they were less than they should have been. The capricious, changing nature of the nation was reflected in their action in seeking an alliance first with one international power, then with another. Hosea focuses upon three aspects of this capricious foreign policy.

First, Israel's foreign policy was characterized as "silly and without sense" (v. 11). Like a bird trapped in a room flits blindly and wildly first in one direction and then in another, so Israel was "like a dove, silly and without sense" (v. 11). The "dove" is rather loosely used in the Old Testament to describe a variety of smaller species of pigeons and is often used as a figure of speech. Here Hosea's figure of speech is that of a fluttering bird, flying in first one direction and then another.

Second, irresponsible conduct brings retributive judgment in history. Continuing to use the dove as a figure of speech, Hosea affirms that the Lord will spread his net over them and "bring them down like birds of the air" (v. 12). It is not easy to pursue a course of noninvolvement in international alliances, but for Israel of the eighth century this was the most likely way to have survived. As Isaiah was to say in Judah during the Egyptian crisis: "In return and rest you shall be saved; in quietness and in trust shall be your strength" (Isa. 30:15).

Third, there is little hope of redemption for those who knowingly stray from the Lord (v. 13). In Israel's entangling foreign alliances, they had "strayed" from the Lord, "they have rebelled against me." "Rebel" is the verb from which the noun "transgression" comes: one connotation of sin is an act of rebellion against the Lord. Also, they have "strayed from me"; a word which means to retreat, flee, depart, stray, wander, flutter. Each word suggests the lack of stability and constancy which ought to characterize one's relationship with the Lord. Again, Hosea returns to the theme of the impossibility of redemption, given the character of Israel's repentance: "I would redeem them, but they speak lies against me" (v. 13). How often are the purposes of God for us so far superior to what our actions will permit him to bring to pass?

IV. Half-baked Religion: A Careless Community, 7:14-16

Although all of life was "religious" and no part of one's experience was viewed apart from its relationship to the Lord, the prophet does focus on specifically "religious" relationships which characterized Israel's experiences with the Lord (7:14-16).

First, misdirected prayer suggests a careless, indifferent attitude toward the Lord (v. 14). Rather than crying to the Lord with their heart, the center of will and volitional decisions according to Old Testament thought, "they wail upon their beds." "Wail" is synonymous with "cry out" and suggests no qualitative difference than to "cry out." The intention of the prophet appears clear, however. For he contrasts crying out to the Lord with those practices associated with the worship of Baal. "Upon their beds" refers to the acts of ritual prostitution which were characteristic of Canaanite Baalism. "Gashing" one's self was associated with ecstatic states achieved in the worship of Baal, or in the case of the prophets of Baal in the Elijah narrative (1 Kings 18:28). Again, compromise and insincerity are evident. Rather than crying out to the Lord with their whole heart; they cry out to Baal and in the process "rebel against me" (v. 14).

Second, misguided loyalty brings derisive destruction (vv. 15-16). Despite the Lord's training and strengthening, Israel turned to Baal. As Hosea later points out, it was the Lord who "taught Ephraim to walk, I took them up in my arms; but they did not know that I healed them" (v. 11:3). "Trained" is the same word (*yasar*) that is translated "chastise" in 7:12 and as "chastiser" or "chastise" in 5:2. Biblically, chastisement has an element of discipline. It is educative and redemptive rather than punitive. It is those whom the Lord loves, whom he chastens. Israel's deception in turning to Baal (v. 16) is well characterized by likening the nation to a "treacherous bow" which does not "shoot straight." One can hardly depend upon a bow that pulls, or on a rifle that is not sighted in properly. Neither can one depend on an individual or a nation whose loyalty is equally lacking in dependability. The "insolence" of compromised people finds its own reward: "derision in the land of Egypt." Egypt was a traditional symbol for bondage. Hosea's point is clear. There is to be a new bondage for those whose insolence (v. 16), treachery (v. 16), evil (v. 15), rebellion (v. 14), lies (v. 13) and misdirected prayer (v. 14) have lead them to a religious experience best described as "half-baked."

6

Reaping the Whirlwind

8:1-14

Hosea establishes a principle later made more specific by the apostle Paul. Most persons are better acquainted with the Pauline emphasis: "Whatever a man sows, that he will also reap" (Gal. 6:7). Not only so, the prophet suggests that one's sin is compounded. One not only reaps what one sows, often he reaps more than he has sown: "For they sow the wind, and they shall reap the whirlwind" (Hos. 8:7). Whether in its prophetic or apostolic form, the principle is equally pertinent. Man's sin sets in process powers of retribution. Like a boomerang, sin turns round upon us with destructive power. There is a moral order operative within history which is as certain in its presence as are the physical laws that govern the operation of the universe. That moral order is not independent of God but is expressive of his character and presence in history.

The general theme of chapter eight is the broken covenant. Israel has broken the relationship created by the covenant into which she had entered with the Lord. There are four subsidiary themes within the overall theme: the broken covenant (1-3), the idol builders (4-7), kingship and foreign alliances (8-10), false worship and fortresses (11-14).

I. Rejecting God, Rejected by God, 8:1-3

The covenant formed the dynamic cement that bound Israel's relationship with the Lord. Out of sheer grace and love, the Lord made a covenant with Israel. As a guide to enable Israel to become in history what covenant relationship suggested that she should be, the Lord also gave his "torah." To break covenant, therefore, was no mere "crime," it was "treason"—the repudiation of one's fundamental basis of relationship. Like an adulterous wife, Israel had broken the vows which sealed her relationship to the Lord. She had "spurned the good" (v. 3), not knowing that the Lord in turn had "spurned your calf, O Samaria" (v. 5). Those who spurn the Lord find that in the same action they have been spurned. It is a dynamic relationship which binds us to the Lord. When this is broken, what is left of life with him?

First, the urgency of the broken covenant rests in the fact that relationship and covenant are intertwined (v. 1). That there is a note of urgency about verse 1 is a generally accepted assumption based on grammatical structure. The language is broken, staccato, lacking imperative verbs: "Upon thy lips a trumpet, like the eagle upon the house of the LORD." Either the text has been obscured in transmission, or it is indicative of agitated speech. This leads one to assume that the chapter begins with the outpoured grief of a prophet. His message becomes a series of sobs in the vortex of his threat directed against his people.

The "trumpet" is one of alarm, associated with the warning given to villages under threat of imminent attack (cf. 5:8; Amos 3:6). "A vulture" may also be translated "*as a* vulture" (cf. RSV, based upon the Hebrew text) and technically suggests "something like a vulture." The vulture (*nesher*) is the griffon-vulture or "eagle"; not the "vulture" with which persons in the United States are generally acquainted (not a buzzard). On occasion, the RSV translates the same word "eagle" (cf. Ezek. 17:3; Prov. 23:5). The word is used as a metaphor for swiftness (Jer. 4:13; 2 Sam. 1:23), dangerous voracity (Hab. 1:8; Prov. 30:17), and majestic superiority (Ezek. 17:3; Ex. 19:4).[1] Wolff further suggests that "house of the LORD" may well be a political reference to Israel, much like the phrase "house of Omri." The advances of Tiglath-Pileser III were well characterized as an eagle circling to hurtle upon Israel (probably in 733 B.C.). A strong argument against interpreting "house of the LORD" as a reference to the Temple is at least twofold: (1) the Temple was in Jerusalem; the oracle is addressed to the Northern Kingdom, and (2) at the time of the Assyrian crisis under Tiglath-Pileser III (745-

---

[1] Wolff, *op. cit.*, p. 137.

727), the Temple was not threatened. The reference suggests the haunting picture of a bird of prey circling over a nation which has violated its relationship with its protector, the Lord.

The motivation for the prophet's threat immediately follows: Israel has "broken my covenant and transgressed my law." "Covenant" is associated with words meaning to bind or to fetter. It was used to describe international treaties during the second millennium B.C., as well as the unique relationship with the Lord and Israel. The word translated "broken" actually means to "pass over" or traverse in the sense of passing beyond or through a land or a city. Also, the word came to mean to overstep or transgress a covenant or command (cf. Num. 14:41; Josh. 7:11,15; Hos. 6:7; 8:1; Isa. 24:5). The picture is clear, Israel has passed over the fetter that bound them to the Lord. The covenant which rests at the heart of both the Old Testament (Covenant) and the New Testament (Covenant) was forsaken.

Also, Israel had "transgressed my law" (v. 1). The words are out of order in the Hebrew text, probably for emphasis. It is against the "law" in the sense of instruction or total revelation of the Lord that Israel rebelled. As Wolff suggests concerning "torah" or "law":

> "This word denotes the entire disclosure of Yahweh's will, already fixed in writing, which goes back to God's own hand (8:12). This disclosure is not a presupposition of the covenant, but a consequence of it. It describes that attitude and conduct appropriate to the covenant (. . . which Hosea mentions in 4:1 f in his allusion to apodictic law. In this respect, the Torah can also mediate the entire 'knowledge of God' (4:6).[2]

"Transgressed" (*pasha'*) refers to an overt act of rebellion. It is often used of the rebellion of one nation against another (1 Kings 12:19; 2 Kings 1:1; 3:5,7), although it is used most often as an act of rebellion against God (Isa. 1:28; 46:8; 53:12; Ps. 51:1).

Second, hypocritical phrases of endearment stand in marked contrast to demonstrated fidelity. The cry in verse 2 was probably used in worship, a cultic cry in which worshipers affirmed devotion to

---

[2] *Op. cit.*, p. 138.

the Lord. Notice the inverted word order, probably for emphasis: "*To me* they cry: My God, we Israel know thee." Like persons in contemporary congregations who "sing the praises of Zion" these ancient worshipers proclaimed their devotion. That their exaltation of the Lord was superficial is apparent in the several indictments which Hosea enumerates.

Third, despite superficial cries of commitment, Israel's actual response to the Lord was one of rejection: "Israel has spurned the good" (v. 3). The "good" may refer to the entirety of Israel's relationship with the Lord: gifts of life, land, community. But the "good" may also refer to that quality of living which the Lord intended to characterize covenant living. The latter possibility is more likely. In this regard, the varied ways in which Amos used "good" is instructive. For example, he appears to equate seeking God and seeking good. Compare Amos 5:6, "Seek the LORD and live," and 5:14, "Seek good . . . that you may live." Israel had spurned those dynamic qualities associated with covenant living: the "good."

The same word used to describe Israel's default of covenant relationships ("spurn") is later used of God's action concerning Israel's object of false worship: "I have spurned your calf, O Samaria" (v. 5). While one's relationship with the Lord is not on the basis of "you do this to me, and I'll do that to you," there is a sense in which we reap what we sow. We spurn the good, and we awaken to discover that in rejecting the good we shared in the rejection of ourselves. Israel rejected the Lord's covenant and the Lord with that covenant, but in so doing they participated in their own rejection: "Rejecting God, Rejected by God."

II. The Idol Builders: Handmade Religion, 8:4-7

Craftsmen normally prize "handmade" crafts, treasuring them above assembly line items. But there is one area in which "handmade" suggests too much of the craftsman. For many, religion is "handmade," crafted to the design of one's conception and fashioned by the skill of one's ingenuity. In other words, it is idolatry.

Hosea insists that Israel made its own kings, its own god(s) (v. 4-6) and in the process had made its own judgment (v. 7). His concerns are handmade kings, handmade gods, and handmade judgment.

First, government was "handmade" in the sense that the Lord had not been involved in the establishment of the kings: "They made kings, but not through me" (v. 4). Hosea may have in mind the rapid overthrow of one king after another. Six kings came to the throne of Israel in approximately fifteen years following the death of Jeroboam II; three within a single year. Or, is it possible that Hosea stands in the old antimonarchial tradition associated with Samuel: a posture which always viewed kingship as less than the divine will? (cf. 1 Sam 8:4 ff). In both instances, kingship came into being apart from the Lord. Kings were Israel's own creation. Monarchy had displaced theocracy. Government had been severed from the dynamic of divine presence.

Second, religion was "handmade" in the sense that idolatry reflects the attempt to create God in one's own image. Although Israel had expended precious silver and gold in making idols, the Lord's anger burns against them (v. 5). He has spurned their idolatrous work, the golden calf at Bethel. Such an idol is not God, "A workman made it" (v. 6).

One of the stronger arguments against idolatry in the Old Testament is its folly: "What profit is an idol when its maker has shaped it, a metal image, a teacher of lies? For the workman trusts in his own creation when he makes dumb idols!" (Hab. 2:18; cf. Isa. 44:9 ff; Jer. 10:3 ff). Man-made religion suffers the same inevitable fate as the golden calf of Israel: "The calf of Samaria shall be broken in pieces" (v. 6). Handmade religion fails: It fails you here and now, it fails you when you need spiritual strength most, it fails you when it is too late to make other provision.

Third, judgment was "handmade" in the sense that it resulted from man's own irresponsible action (v. 7). One might well translate the preposition "for" as an interjection: "O how they sow the wind and reap the whirlwind!" The deed of judgment is inherent in the seed of rebellion. But more than merely reaping what one sows is involved here. As Wolff suggests, the law of correspondence as well as multiplication applies to this wisdom saying.

Not only is judgment so often in "like kind," it is also compounded.

"The wind" (rauach) may be used of breath (Job 9:18) or a gentle breeze (cf. Gen. 3:8), although it also is used of a rushing wind (Ps. 55:8) or a storm wind (Ps. 107:25). The word translated "whirlwind" (suphah), on the other hand, consistently means a "storm-wind." The implications are patently clear: principles of correspondence and multiplication suggest that man creates his own judgment, sowing the inevitable harvest as he plants the seed of rebellion and irresponsibility. Yet from the biblical perspective, such an emphasis should not be permitted to eradicate the dynamic presence of God in the manifestation of judgment through historical processes. God is at work in history. In both the seed sown and the harvest reaped, his providence affirms his abiding presence.

Judgment described by Hosea is two-fold. First, the harvest has failed, "The standing grain has no heads," crop failures being a common means of symbolizing judgment in prophetic literature (Amos 4:9 f; Hag. 1:9). Second, an invader will enter the land to devour any grain that is produced (v. 7).

III. Guaranteeing One's Own Future, Through Kingship and Foreign Alliances, 8:8-10

King Hoshea's submission to Tiglath-Pileser III in 733 b.c. forms the focus of Hosea's concern for Israel. In a play on words between the statement that "aliens would devour (bala')" the grain (v. 7), Hosea suggests that Israel is already "swallowed up (bala')." Having broken covenant relationships with the Lord, Israel sought to guarantee her own freedom by entering into a submissive role with Assyria. Adultery and promiscuity are reprehensible enough, but Israel's role is less than either: "Ephraim has hired lovers" (v. 9). Israel is reduced to a state less than harlotry—she now is forced to pay her "lovers." Although Hosea's figures of speech are repelling, they are graphically accurate. Those who seek to guarantee their own future apart from the Lord are guilty of more than adultery. Whether ancient or modern, no nation can long endure when dominated by such a foreign policy: "They shall cease for a little while from anointing kings and princes" (v. 10).

IV. False Worship and Insecure Fortresses, 8:11-14

The superficiality of Israel's worship and faith are central to the prophet's message. Hosea's people multiplied places of worship but had no vital relationship with the Lord. They multiplied their national defenses, but they had no assurance of peace and protection from without. Superficial to the extreme, both worship and faith were lacking in vitality.

First, the numerical multiplication of places of worship fails to guarantee a dynamic relationship with the Lord (v. 11). As Harold Cooke Phillips once suggested, when one seeks to evaluate religious experience, the question is "not how many but what sort." Altars were designed to effect meeting with the Lord. Yet, in the time of Hosea, they had become places for sin. They had been used too long for the wrong motives and for equally wrong ends (cf. Hos. 4:7). Even the best can become the worst. How strange that the means whereby sin might have been atoned for became the means whereby sin was created. Is there not the continuing danger of this same polarization in contemporary religious life? May not the best become the worst when its meaning is abused? When one recognizes that all of this happened to Israel in a time when people multiplied the number of altars in the land, it leads one to observe that in contemporary circles we may well have reached the time when we should stop counting Christians and start weighing them. The fundamental question, again, is not quantity, but quality.

Second, contradicting the religious activity of the era was the negation of revelation by Hosea's generation (v. 12). In a graphic use of hyperbole, Hosea suggests that if the laws of the Lord were written "by ten thousands, they would be regarded a strange thing" (v. 12). It is not enough to *know* the will of God, believers are to *do* the will of God.

Third, delight in the formalities of worship guarantees neither the Lord's presence nor his approval (v. 13). Sacrifices were no burden for Israel of Hosea's day: "They love sacrifice" (v. 13). Because of this, Israel was to return to a state of being prior to the covenant: life in Egypt (v. 13) symbolizing bondage like that which Israel knew prior to the Exodus experience.

Fourth, forgetting the Lord leads one to place his reliance in works of his own creation; in this instance, "palaces" and fortified cities" (v. 14). To "forget" means far more than a lapse of memory.[3] Forgetting the Lord or the covenant suggests gross hypocrisy, even apostasy. Words such as *hear, remember,* and *forget* are characterized by overtones of psychic meaning far more significant than the merely physical functions of memory. Although the word translated "palaces" may also mean "temple," the context suggests the RSV translation "palaces." Israel and Judah have built *palaces* which have become the source of their strength: palaces and fortified cities; not the Lord!

Such action as that described by Hosea goes neither unnoticed nor unpunished in history by the Lord. Not only does the Lord have no "delight" in the hypocrisy of Israel's worship (v. 13), he will "remember their iniquity"—suggesting that the Lord will do more than call it to mind. He will "punish their sins; they shall return to Egypt" (v. 13). The certainty of the Lord's action is clearly indicated (v. 14). Hebrew verbs specify no sense of time as do verbs in Greek or English. They indicate "complete" or "incomplete" action, whether in past, present, or future time. Here, the prophet uses "perfect" verbs indicating completed action. Judged by the context, the judgment is obviously future. But Hosea describes it as having already come to pass. Specifically, "I have sent a fire upon his cities, and it has devoured his strongholds" (v. 14).

---

[3] Cf. comments on Hos. 4:6 *supra.*, p. 28.

7

Then, What Will You Do?

9:1-17

"What will you do on the day of the appointed festival, and on the day of the feast of the LORD?" inquired the prophet Hosea (9:5). The prophet's underlying assumption is that there will come a day when people will be at complete loss concerning an appropriate course of action in the midst of overwhelming contrary circumstances. The picture portrayed by the prophet is one of absolute bewilderment as people confront the enormity of their historical predicament. Hosea saw the time when exile would preclude the joy of festival days, the solemn worship of the Lord at the high places, the undergirding confidence of God's unbroken presence. What, indeed, does one do when there is no joy, no worship, no assured presence of the Lord?

The piercing cry of the prophet might well become the wail of every distressed generation. What will we do on *that* day—the day of reckoning? Every generation would do well to hear the words of Hosea experientially: "What will *you* do on the day of appointed festival, and on the day of the feast of the Lord?" What will you do in the death of joy (9:1-6), the denial of revelation (9:7-9), the destruction of communion (9:10-14), and the dissolution of identity (9:15-17)?

I. The Death of Joy, 9:1-6

Life without joy is a contradiction of that quality of life attendant to covenant relationship. Yet, Hosea declared that joy was inappropriate for Israel: "Rejoice not, O Israel!" (v. 1). Historically, Israel had been called to worship God with joy and enthusiasm: as, for example, in the case of the psalmist: "Be glad in the Lord, and rejoice, O righteous, and shout for joy, all you upright in heart"

59

(Ps. 32:11; cf., Pss. 14:7; 16:9; Joel 2:21,23; Zeph. 3:14). Why then did Hosea call for the cessation of joy?

First, circumstances forbade rejoicing (v. 1). Judgment was imminent, the invader was close at hand. Such a time of national crisis was no time to rejoice. Circumstances were not conducive to joy.

But far more than this was involved in the prohibition of joy. Israel had introduced elements of Canaanite worship into the Lord's worship. The "exulting" which Hosea describes was a characteristic feature of Canaanite nature religion rather than an expression of joy in the historical acts of the Lord. Wolff suggests that the "exultation" was characterized by shrill, unrestrained screams, characteristically moving toward a climax (cf. 7:14). Dorothea Ward Harvey concludes in an article entitled "Rejoice Not, O Israel!" that the term *gil* ("exult," v. 1) seems to be associated with Canaanite ritual in the Old Testament.[1] What Hosea condemns is the appropriation of non-Israelite patterns of worship. Israel has forsaken the Lord, playing the harlot, loving a "harlot's hire." Such joy as she had in these experiences are far from the joy which the biblical writers associated with the Lord's action in history. Irreligious joy, joy devoid of the Lord's presence is precluded for the people of God. There is no place for riotous joy grounded in ways of life or thought contrary to the Lord's revelation. It is this quality of joy which is to die in Israel, not legitimate rejoicing in the Lord.

Second, those who rejoice and exult in realities other than the Lord will be forsaken (vv. 2-3). Previously Hosea described the gifts of the land as the hire of a harlot; gifts which Israel accepted from Baal, not recognizing that it was the Lord who provided them (cf. 2:8 ff). The threshing floor and the winevat shall fail Israel. Her "gifts" will be taken from her (cf. 2:9 ff). Those who become so insensitive to the Lord that they can no longer discern the gifts of God will eventually forfeit those same gifts.

Also, in addition to the loss of the "hire" which she had associated with Baal, Israel will lose her heritage, the land: "They shall not

---

[1] "Rejoice Not, O Israel," in *Israel's Prophetic Heritage*, ed. by Bernard W. Anderson and Walter Harrelson (New York: Harper & Brothers, 1962), pp. 110-128.

remain in the land of the Lord" (v. 3). What God gives, God can take away. Those who have been led out of "Egypt" can be led again to bondage.

Third, those who become insensitive to the Lord and the reality of his gifts forfeit positive qualities of worship (v. 4). For ancient Israelites, exile from the land was equivalent to exile from God and the benefits of worship (cf. David, 1 Sam. 26:19; Naaman, 2 Kings 5:17; Jonah, Jonah 1:3). Hence, in exile it would not be possible to worship the Lord (v. 4). Both wine and bread played important parts in Israelite worship, and the inability to offer them portrayed a comparable inability to worship the Lord in normative patterns. Hosea sought to emphasize the inability of religion as practiced outside Israel to meet the needs of the worshiping community. To be sure, once exile was effected, the people found that the worship of the Lord was not limited by geographical or political boundaries. Using the patterns of thought common to his day, however, Hosea stressed that one facet of Israel's judgment was the forfeiture of normative patterns of worship. Exile did not mean the loss of God, but it did mean that meaningful aspects of religious life and worship were forfeited. The meaning of worship is eroded by the faithless incorporation of heretical conceptions of God into patterns of worship. What one believes affects how one worships.

Fourth, a mood of futility characterizes those who abandon the Lord for competitive religious conceptions (vv. 5-6). In a rhetorical question, Hosea poses the futility of that day of calamity when Israel forfeits her heritage as a covenant people: "What will you do on the day . . .?" (v. 5). The implication is clear. They will be unable to worship on the "day of the appointed festival"—possibly the fall harvest festival. What will you do *then?* Then it is too late when "nettles" have grown up over your idols, and "thorns" have grown over the places where the religious pilgrims pitched their tents; too late then to right the wrongs of another generation or an era in your own generation. There is a finality about judgment in history which precludes reversal of the situation. One can only ask an open-ended question in rhetorical form: "Then, what will you do . . .?" What indeed shall one do when the established forms of worship are abandoned or lost, when one's relationship with the Lord is compromised, when the heritage of a land and a nation expires—what shall one do when it is too late?

II. The Denial of Revelation, or the Foolishness of Preaching, 9:7-9

The "festival speech" (vv. 1-7a) was probably spoken by Hosea during a time of festival at one of the religious centers in Israel (cf. Amos 7:10 ff). The change of pronouns from second person to third person which are found in verses 1-9 suggest that an actual debate or argument takes place, with prophet and people interchanging comments, together with the priests. Within this type context, one is able to identify more clearly with the accusations brought against the prophet (v. 7), together with his response (vv. 8-9).

First, recompense is a reality; Hosea reaffirms the dire calamity of abandoning the revelation of God for the worship of Baal, (v. 7a). One cannot abandon the Lord with impunity: "The days of punishment have come, the days of recompense have come." Although the context suggests that the judgment is future, the prophet is so certain of its appearance that he describes it as having already come; a confidence grounded in the prophet's certainty concerning the nature and character of God. To convey this conception, the prophet used Hebrew verbs suggesting completed action: literally, "they have already come."

Second, revelation through the prophet is revoked by the people (v. 7b). Response to the revelation mediated through the prophet was both angry and demeaning: "The prophet is a fool, the man of the spirit is mad" (v. 7b). Prophets of any generation are liable to be written off as "fools" and "mad" when the content of their message is inconsistent with prevalent practices by the people. The prophet acceptable to the masses is well characterized by Micah: "If a man should go about and utter wind and lies, saying, 'I will preach to you of wine and strong drink,' he would be the preacher for this people!" (Mic. 2:11). In contemporary terms, a prophet like the one described by Micah would "get a unanimous call." But the canonical prophets of the eighth century, B.C. were not like this. Rather, like William Loyd Garrison, the antislavery crusader of a century ago, they were as harsh as truth and as uncompromising as justice. They did not equivocate, they did not retreat a single inch—and ultimately the world did hear them. But the world of their day did not want to hear them. For such a world, Hosea and his counterparts were "fools" and madmen.

"Fool" (*'ewil*) is a word which appears nineteen times in the book of Proverbs. The "fool" despises wisdom and discipline (Prov. 1:7; 15:5) and is a quarrelsome fellow (20:3). He is a "foolish talker" (Prov. 10:8,10). He is a "blockhead," and it is foolish and useless to try and instruct him (16:22; 27:22). "Man of the spirit" (cf. Elijah, 1 Kings 18:12; Micaiah ben Imlah, 1 Kings 22:21 f; Elisha, 2 Kings 2:9) is probably a synonym for "man of God," a common designation of the prophet in the Northern Kingdom.

Why do people respond to prophets in this manner? Hosea suggests two reasons: iniquity and hatred. Because of the character of their own lives, people cannot bear exposure and condemnation. When truth becomes relevant to one's sin, self-defense dictates that the prophet be discredited as a fool and a madman. Second, the "great hatred" of the people for a prophet who interpreted both history and the lives of the people in the light of God led them to discredit the prophet by assassinating his character. As Amos earlier had suggested of the same generation in Israel, "They hate him who reproves in the gate, and they abhor him who speaks the truth" (Amos 5:10 ff). When the lives of persons are characterized by "iniquity" and governed by "hatred," one should hardly be surprised that they discredit the revelation of God mediated through the prophet; declaring those who declare the word of the Lord to be both "fools" and "mad."

Third, the role of the prophet is reaffirmed by Hosea: "The prophet is the watchman of Ephraim" (v. 8). Hosea established a conception of the prophetic office echoed by both Jeremiah (6:17) and Ezekiel (3:17; 33:2,6). The prophet scans history, warning the people of impending doom, certain that his own life will be either validated or condemned according to the fidelity with which he fulfills his role (cf. Ezek. 33:2 ff). Although the prophet has the *function* of watchman over the people of God, his *fate* is to be entrapped and

hated—even "in the house of his God" (v. 8). To the credit of faithful
prophets across the centuries, their fate has not precluded the fulfillment of their function. The vindication of the prophet is bound
up with God: "He will remember their [the people] iniquity, he
will punish their sins" (v. 9). Prophets of every generation do well
to leave vindication with God, rather than assuming responsibility
for self-vindication. Jeremiah's counsel is altogether appropriate:
"But, O LORD of hosts, who judgest righteously . . . to thee have
I committed my cause" (Jer. 11:20).

III. The Destruction of Communion, 9:10-14

Communion with the Lord was initiated through the covenant
relationship into which Israel entered with the Lord during the
wilderness experience. It was in the wilderness that the Lord found
Israel "like the first fruit on the fig tree" (v. 10). But no sooner
had the Lord led his people through the wilderness to the verge
of the Promised Land, to Baal-peor (cf. Num. 25:1 ff), than they
began to play the harlot with the *ba'al* of Peor. Israel's infidelity
is no new development; it is, rather, ingrained into her historical
existence. From the beginning she has "played the harlot." Because
of this, her "glory shall fly away like a bird" (v. 11 ff).

Glory suggests the "weight" or significance of a person. When
used of God, it becomes a way of speaking of God's presence, of
God himself. In a time when belief in the transcendence of God
precluded the conception of God himself appearing, biblical writers
used the "glory of God" as a way of speaking of God's "burning
presence." In the passage at hand, Hosea figuratively describes Israel's
glory in terms of the birth of children; a common way of describing
God's blessing in the Old Testament. But for Israel there is to be
no births (vv. 11-14). They have lost the "glory" (v. 11); they forfeited
the presence of God.

There is no abiding glory for man apart from relationship with
the Lord. It is his presence that becomes the touch of glory. Glory
comes in the depth of one's communion with the Lord in covenant
relationships, and the measure of that depth of communion becomes
the measure of the glory that one experiences in life. Man cannot

find authentic existence apart from this "touch of glory"—the reality of a Presence, unseen but sure, incomprehensible yet known in mystery. For those who have experienced the loss of glory, as did ancient Israel, the question of Wordsworth is perennially appropriate: "Where is it now, the glory and the dream?"

IV. The Dissolution of Identity, 9:15-17

Does "Gilgal" (v. 15) suggest an attack on kingship, since the first king was enthroned there (cf. 1 Sam. 11:14); or is it an attack on worship, since Gilgal was a primitive site of worship (cf. Josh. 4:19 ff)? Although the evidence is inconclusive, reference to "princes" (v. 15) and to the political fortunes of the nation (v. 17) imply an attack on kingship. Again, the dissolution of national identity is not a new phenomenon. It had its beginning as early as Gilgal. Sin is no temporary and relatively insignificant occurrence; it is deeply ingrained in historical existence, reaching far back into the realm of the community of faith. This is not to excuse a given generation. But it is to suggest that one wrestles with powers far greater and farther reaching than a personal failure.

Through a variety of figures of speech, Hosea makes clear the fact that national identity is to be forfeited; dissolved in the sea of history. For example, the Lord will "drive them out of my house. I will love them no more" (v. 15). Ephraim shall bear no fruit; and even if children should be born they will be slain in warfare (v. 16). A nation so callous and insensitive as to reject the loving relationship provided with the Lord through the covenant will become a vagabond nation; without roots: "My God will cast them off . . . they shall be wanderers among the nations" (v. 17, cf. the analogy of Cain, Gen. 4:16). People whose identity was created through relationship with the Lord may anticipate that the rupture of that relationship will result in the dissolution of the identity created by the relationship in the first place.

8

The Time Is Right!

10:1-15

There are characteristic features of every generation which lead one to observe that within a particular era, "It was the best of times and the worst of times." There were many characteristics of Hosea's generation to suggest that it was the "best of times" in Israel. One might observe, for example, that the emergence of prophets like Amos and Hosea in the eighth century B.C. were adequate evidence to prove that it was a time of unique insight and revelation of the will and purposes of God. On a more superficial plane, but one which weighed heavily with Israel as with all persons, was the prosperity which characterized that era. Also, religion flourished; crowds thronged the sanctuaries, sacrifices and offerings filled the altars, music resounded across the countryside. It was the best of times.

But it was also the worst of times. Although prophets like Amos and Hosea appeared as a testimony to the Lord's continuing revelation, they were rejected by the masses; certainly by established functionaries of religion. Amos was banished to Judah (Amos 7:12 ff). Hosea was written off as a "fool" and a "madman" (Hos. 9:7). Prosperity was everywhere apparent. But from a careful reading of the prophets, one finds that wealth had been accumulated by the few at the expense of the many; and this through social oppression (cf. Amos 2:6 ff; 4:1 ff; 8:4 ff). People did fill the places of worship. Worshipers loved to sacrifice, and the external formalities of worship prospered (Hos. 8:11 ff; Amos 4:4 ff; 5:21 ff). But the most superficial reading of the prophets reveals that hypocrisy and superficiality characterized worship of that era (cf. Hos. 4:4 ff; 5:1 ff; 8:11 ff; 9:1 ff; Amos 5:21 ff). From quite another perspective, it was the worst of times.

The books of Amos and Hosea reveal that during the mid-eighth century B.C. it was both "the best of times and the worst of times" in Israel. But more significant than this, it was "time to seek the LORD, that he may come and rain salvation upon you" (v. 12). Even the worst of times may become the best of times if the dire circumstances which compose the "worst of times" lead one to repentance and renewal of one's relationships with the Lord. This is the theme of Hosea reflected in the tenth chapter: the time is right for Israel to seek the Lord. Two primary themes form the basic thrust of Hosea's concern reflected in this chapter: broken altars (10:1-8) and broken nation (10:9-15).

I. Shattered Altars: When Religious Systems Crash, 10:1-8

The altars of Israel are to be shattered. Despite their multiplication (8:11) and their "improvement" (10:1), they have become a place for sin (8:11) rather than redemption. In describing the shattering of the altars in Israel, Hosea describes the misuse of prosperity (vv. 1-2) as well as the misuse and abuse of religious systems (vv. 3-8).

First, prosperity had been misused and abused through the multiplication and improvement of false places of worship (10:1-2). The *abundance* of Israel's prosperity is graphically reflected in the prophet's figurative language: "Israel is a luxuriant vine that yields its fruit" (v. 1). In both Isaiah's parable of the vineyard (Isa. 5:1 ff) and in the psalmist's allegorical use of the vine to symbolize Israel in the eightieth psalm (Ps. 80:7 ff), Israel is characterized as a vine planted by the Lord. The luxuriant character of Israelite life during the eighth century B.C. is reflected not only in prophetic literature such as Hosea and Amos but also in the historical narratives of 2 Kings, as well as in archaeological discoveries such as the ivory inlays discovered at Samaria.

Israel's *abuse of her prosperity* is reflected in the extensive building programs related to the altars which combined the Lord's worship with that of Baal. There was nothing intrinsically wrong with building an altar, so long as the altar remained an appropriate channel for the grace and power of the Lord. But Israel's altars had become places of sinning (Hos. 8:11), a place of which the Lord might say:

"I hate, I despise your feasts, and I take no delight in your solemn assemblies" (Amos 5:21). Israel's expenditures upon the increase and improvement of altars was in direct proportion to the improvement of the economy: "The more his fruit increased the more altars he built" (v. 1).

In contrast to the portrait of Israel which the frenzied building and improvement of altars suggested, the *actual condition of Israel's heart* negated any positive characteristics which may have appeared to have accompanied the building and improving of altars. "Their heart is false" (v. 2). The heart, according to Old Testament patterns of thought, was the center of intellect, the locus for volitional decisions, the center of personality, the essence of the person. This integral aspect of Hebrew personality was "false." The word translated "false" (*chalag*) means to be divided (I), but it also means to be smooth or slippery (II). In this instance, it probably means slippery or smooth in the sense of faithlessness or deceptive. People with "slippery hearts" must "bear their guilt." The Lord's *action against deceptive worshipers* is clear. He will "break down their altars, and destroy their pillars" (v. 2). Religious systems built by people with slippery, deceptive hearts will shatter themselves on the anvil of history.

Second, religion had been misused and abused by otherwise sincere people (vv. 3-8). There is no suggestion that Israelite worshipers deliberately set out to misuse and abuse religion or religious experiences. It is never so deliberate and specific as this. Rather, in the course of what may seem to be appropriate to a mistaken people, the character of religious experience is warped and twisted until in actual fact religion is both misused and abused by the worshiper. Doubtless, worshipers of Hosea's generation saw nothing wrong with combining features of Baalism with the worship of the Lord; no more than contemporary persons deliberately set out to compromise and adulterate contemporary religious life. But thoroughly sincere persons may be thoroughly wrong. As the writer of Proverbs reminds the reader, "There is a way that seems right to a man, but its end is the way to death" (Prov. 14:12).

Forces within history are at work in such manner as to bring to an end a people who so misuse and abuse their covenant relationships. Hosea sees the time when the people will have no king; nor will they any longer have any confidence that a king could deliver them (v. 3). Perhaps for the first time the prophet injects a glimmer of hope; however negative it may appear to be. But there is hope for people who speak out of the extremity of their need to admit that their situation cannot be remedied by human action— and the establishment of successive dynasties had been the action of men, not of God. Perhaps the people would come to that time when they saw that kingship depended upon the charismatic word of the Lord; not upon palace intrigues such as those described by Hosea (cf. 7:3 ff). Because political agreements made with newly installed kings have been "mere words; . . . empty oaths," judgment has sprung up in their midst like weeds in the furrow of a field (v. 4).

In such a time of calamity, the people of Samaria shall mourn for the calf at Bethel; sarcastically referred to by Hosea as Beth-aven, house of iniquity rather than house of God (v. 5). Hosea uses a foreign word, also found in Zephaniah 1:4 and 2 Kings 23:5, to characterize the faithless priests of Israel, the "Idolatrous priests." Their wailing is described by the use of the same word which appears in 9:1, "Exult not like the peoples." Apparently, this particular kind of wailing was characteristic of worship associated with Baal. Disdaining to refer to the golden calf, Hosea says that "the thing shall be carried to Assyria" (v. 6) as tribute to Tiglath-Pileser III, the "great king." Kingship shall perish, thorn and thistle shall grow up on the abandoned altars on which Israel had expended her prosperity. In such a time of shame and catastrophe, the people "shall say to the mountains, Cover us, and to the hills, Fall upon us" (v. 8).

When religious systems created by men have been shattered and devastation is so great as that described by the prophet, the "time is right" to return to the Lord for renewal and healing.

II. War: The Fruit of False Trust, 10:9-15

War is the fruit of false trust: "Because you have trusted in your chariots and in the multitude of your warriors, therefore the tumult of war shall arise among your people" (vv. 13,14). Hosea links

together three oracles, each loosely related to the theme of warfare
such as that which characterized the Assyrian advance of the mid-
eighth century and following: a time of discipline (vv. 9-10), a time
to return to the Lord (vv. 11-12), a time to reap the result of false
trust (vv. 13-15).

First, crises such as warfare may be disciplinary when interpreted
from the perspective of faith (vv. 9-10). Israel's sin is as old as events
at Gibeah; perhaps the case of the slaying of the Levite's concubine
at Gibeah (Judg. 19:1 ff) or the civil war which this precipitated
(Judg. 20 to 21). Perhaps Hosea sees judgment returned in like kind
as war returns to Gibeah: "Shall not war overtake them in Gibeah?"
(v. 9). Gibeah previously had been cited as one of those villages
in which the trumpet of alarm had been sounded (5:8). Twice in
a single verse the prophet interprets this catastrophe as a time of
chastisement—a disciplinary time when the people might learn from
the agony of their experience (v. 10). The word translated "chastise"
and "chastised" (v. 10) is identical with the previous uses in 5:2,
"I will chastise all of them," and in 7:15, "I *trained* and strengthened
their arms." Again, Israel's sin is not new, the passing offense of
the moment. It is firmly grounded in history, as ingrained as the
events which occurred early in her history at Gibeah. Nations, as
individuals, do reap what they sow—and more. So, at Gibeah, site
of the early offenses, Israel will be chastised for her "double iniquity."

Second, crises may confront one with an awareness of need which
would otherwise go unnoticed; turning crisis into a time to return
to the Lord (vv. 11-12). Israel is compared to a trained heifer who
had the light task of threshing grain; trampling out chaff from grain
on a threshing floor. Her owner had "spared her fair neck" (v. 11).
So Israel also had enjoyed a favored position. But the time had come
when Israel must be put to the yoke and do the common work
assigned to any other draft animal (v. 11). The passage begins in
such fashion as to suggest a judgment speech, but with verse 12
there is introduced a salvation oracle. For Israel is called upon to
sow righteousness; that is, conformity to the covenant relationships
she sustains with the Lord and members of the covenant community.
She is to reap fruit "according to steadfast love"; that is, what she
reaps will be in keeping with the steadfast love which characterizes

her relationships in the covenant. These two qualities, righteousness and steadfast love, are uniquely related to covenant relationship. They are among those words which epitomize faithful relationships with the Lord and other persons in the covenant community. Not only in the negative sense of judgment do we "reap what we sow" but also in the positive dimension of salvation as well. Those who sow righteousness and steadfast love will reap salvation from the Lord. Hosea argues that in the worst of times, when burdens are heaviest, nights longest, and situations the most uncertain—at that precise time is "the time to seek the Lord" (v. 12).

Third, crises may be the result of false trust; Israel's time of warfare was: "Because you have trusted in your chariots . . . therefore the tumult of war shall arise" (vv. 13-15). In a statement which presents another aspect of reaping what one sows, Hosea indicates that because Israel had "plowed iniquity, you have reaped injustice, you have eaten the fruit of lies" (v. 13). Although the call to sow righteousness and steadfast love is paramount in its claim upon those in the covenant relation, Israel has sown a different seed: iniquity. They have reaped the opposite of righteousness: injustice. In clarifying Israel's action, Hosea points out that they have trusted, felt secure in, their military armaments: chariots and warriors. The scene closes with Israel engaged in battle, although identification of the foe is no longer possible: the time when "Shalman destroyed Beth-arbel" (v. 14). The reference is probably to Salamanu of Moab, although some take this as a reference to Shalmaneser V (727-722 B.C.). The essential message of the passage is clear, whatever the specific historical event may have been: False trust leads to war. Trust (v. 13) should be directed toward the Lord; however, Israel may have misdirected her trust on a variety of different occasions.

In summary, chapter 10 describes Israel as prosperous and luxuriant, spending resources on the extension and improvement of her places of worship (v. 1-2). It seemed to be the best of times. Actually, it was the worst of times for the religious system, her "altars," were about to crash (vv. 3-8), warfare was imminent (vv. 9-15). But it was precisely in what was both the "best of times and the worst of times" that Hosea insisted that the time was right to seek the Lord.

9
How Does the Lord Love Thee?
11:1-12

Words made immortal by Elizabeth Barrett Browning are strangely pertinent for Hosea's moving appeal grounded in God's love for his people:

"How do I love thee? Let me count the ways.
I love thee to the depth and breadth and height
My soul can reach, when feeling out of sight
For the ends of Being and ideal Grace.
I love thee to the level of everyday's
Most quiet need, by sun and candlelight.
I love thee freely, as men strive for Right;
I love thee purely, as they turn from Praise.
I love thee with the passion put to use
In my old griefs, and with my childhood's faith."

How does the Lord love thee? Oh, says Hosea, let me count the ways. He loved you when he called you to sonship (vv. 1-2). He loved you when you were insensitive and rejected his love (vv. 3-4). When you abandoned him, he still loved you and loves you still (vv. 5-7). He loved you with a compassionate agony that would not give you up (vv. 8-9). He loved you with persistence that brought you back to your relationship of love with him.

I. God Loved You When He Called You into Sonship, 11:1,2

Love was the theme of the Lord's relationship with Israel. There was no other explanation for her existence than his grace, his unmerited love in action: not Israel's genius for religion, for others were religious also; not her strength, for others were stronger; not her potential, for others also possessed amazing potential. The biblical writer made this clear in explaining Israel's unique relationship to

the Lord: "It was not because you were more in number than any
other people that the LORD set his love upon you and choose you,
for you were the fewest of all peoples; but it is because the LORD
loves you . . . that the LORD has brought you out with a mighty
hand, and redeemed you" (Deut. 7:7,8). It was this quality of unmerited love that called Israel into existence at the time of the Exodus.
The personal, warm relationship between the Lord and Israel is
graphic in the NEB translation "When Israel was a boy, I loved
him; I called my son out of Egypt" (v. 1). The people of God in
every generation form the family of God because of his love and
grace. We are sons and daughters, brothers and sisters together in
faith, because he first loved us and called us unto himself. How
does the Lord love his people?—when he calls them into a family
relationship of love.

But there is a second Old Testament theme which is also fundamental to Hosea's message: the theme of the stubborn son (cf.
Deut. 21:18-21; Isa. 1:2 ff). Like a rebellious son who will obey
neither his father nor his mother (Deut. 21:18), Israel rejected the
Lord's love. Calling the name of a family member is a sure, personal
expression of relationship. To enter the door after coming home
from work and call, "Roy Lee," "Mary Anne," affirms a relationship
grounded in love and cemented in community. But when the Lord
calls, how often do we turn a deaf ear: "The more I called them,
the more they went from me" (v. 2). Rejecting the Lord, Israel turned
to the new gods of Canaan: "they kept sacrificing to the Baals"
(v. 2). But note this: the Lord did not cease to call them, despite
their failure to respond; "the more I called them." How does the
Lord love his people?—when he calls them into a family relationship
of love, and keeps on loving them despite their rejection.

II. God Loved You When You Were Insensitive to His Loving Care, 11:3-4

Hosea sketches a familiar family scene to depict God's loving care:
"Yet it was I who taught Ephraim to walk, I took them up in my
arms" (v. 3). What parent has not taken his or her child by the
fingers, teaching him to walk? There are fewer pictures which more

graphically portray both a parent's loving care and a child's complete
dependence. Or, what parent has not demonstrated love and kindness
by taking a child up in his arms? This is the way of loving parents.
It is no less the way of a loving God who cares and provides for
his children.

Despite this dynamic expression of love and identification, "They
did not know that I healed them" (v. 3). How insensitive each of
us can become to the Lord's grace. Like a parent teaching a child
to walk, or taking the child up in his arms, the Lord loves us. But
we do not know who he is! This theme appeared earlier in Hosea's
indictment of Israel for receiving the gifts of God but ascribing them
to Baal (cf. 2:8). Are we any less insensitive? Do we confuse the
ultimate source of our blessing as did ancient Israel? Do we reject
the loving care of God as have others before us?

Despite the fact that "they did not know," Hosea affirms that
the Lord "led them with cords of compassion, with the bands of
love" (v. 4). Utilizing a picture from the life of the teamster, Hosea
stresses the way in which God had cared for his people. He compares
God's action to one who eases the yoke for the oxen—possibly after
a "hard pull," bending down to them and feeding them (v. 4).
Although the figures of speech are outdated for those living in a
society where there are no longer draft animals such as these, the
character of God described by those figures of speech has not been
outdated. For when the load is heavy and the way is long, the Lord
still "eases the yoke," caring for the needs of his people. How does
the Lord love you? The Lord loves you even when you are insensitive
to his loving care.

III. God Loved You When You Turned Away from Him, 11:5-7

Does there come a time when even love abandons its own? No,
not if one means to imply an arbitrary action whereby the Lord
no longer loves his people. Yes, if one assumes that a people can
become so "bent on turning away" (v. 7) that abandonment is the
inevitable outcome of their action, as well as the means used by
the Lord to bring about return. Earlier Hosea stressed this point:
the Lord will abandon his people "until they acknowledge their

guilt and seek my face, and in their distress they seek me" (5:15). Paul also touched on this in his suggestion that in the face of the debauchery and godlessness of those who failed to respond affirmatively to the Lord, "God gave them up" (cf. Rom. 1:24,26,28). At this juncture, there is a needed but brief distinction to be made. God may give a person up to man's own lusts and godlessness, if this is man's chosen way, but God never gives up on a man.

The prophet describes "love abandoning," abandoning the persons of his love and devotion to the ravages of history. They shall return to bondage (Egypt); "Assyria shall be their king" (v. 5). The sword, symbol of destruction in battle, will "rage against their cities, consume the bars of their gates, and devour them in their fortresses" (v. 6). Places of false refuge will fail when the day of reckoning arrives. And why is all of this happening? Because Israel had refused to return to the Lord (v. 5), they were "bent on turning away from me" (v. 6). Love without power and justice may degenerate into an insipid sentimentality. But the Lord's love is not like this. It possesses both justice and power. Given these qualities love can and does abandon its own—if abandonment is the only way in which both justice and reconciliation can be effected. Viewed solely from the human perspective, the Lord abandons his people to the fortunes of history. How, then, does the Lord love his people? He loves them even when they turn away from him and he abandons them.

IV. God Loved You with a Compassion That Would Not Give You Up, 11:8,9

This passage is one of the more anthropomorphic of the prophet's characterizations of the Lord. He depicts the Lord recoiling with a compassion that "grows warm and tender" (v. 8). Yet, as Wheeler Robinson once suggested, there is more than an anthropomorphism involved here. The question Robinson poses is fundamentally this: is the Lord merely described as having feeling like a man, or does God actually suffer? Robinson affirms that God does suffer, that suffering is a fundamental characteristic of the Lord. While a view of God as one who cannot suffer is much more manageable for theology, says Robinson, it is also a view which is "very high and dry."

The thought of abandoning his people (vv. 6-7) precipitates an anguish in the heart of God: "How can I give you up, O Ephraim!" (8). No matter what a son has done, how can a father give him up? As a father once rationalized his continued support of a son who had long been a source of disappointment, "But preacher, he's still my boy!" Something strangely akin to this surely beats strongly in the heart of God. This is love in agony: how can the Lord make those whom he loves like Admah and Zeboim, cities of the plain destroyed together with Sodom and Gomorrah? The heart of God recoils. His compassion grows warm and tender (v. 8).

Love that agonizes with compassion and tenderness finds a way: "I will not execute my fierce anger" (v. 9). It is not the Lord's purpose to obliterate his people, only to chasten and discipline them in the crucible of national suffering. Stated otherwise, within the framework of history, the judgment of God is redemptive rather than punitive. The *fierce* anger of God would suggest obliteration, but this he will not execute. He comes to deliver, not to destroy (v. 8).

Why is this so? Given the faithlessness and infidelity of Israel, why should she be spared? Having experienced the adulterous conduct of a promiscuous wife such as Gomer, why not drive her out? Because of who God is, grace prevails over law, love over hate, and discipline over destruction: "I am God and not man" (v. 9). By any human standard, any one of us has "sinned away his day of grace." But thank God, the Lord does not treat us like we treat one another. Action grounded in such grace and love is possible because it springs out of the character of God. Because of who God is there is ground for hope, even for the worst of us. This is how God loves—with a compassion that will not give up on us.

V. God Loved You with a Persistence That Brought You Back to Him, 11:10-12

Love's victory is clearly reflected in the picture of Israel responding to the Lord's action. This is love triumphant. While Israel previously was "bent on turning away from" the Lord (v. 7), now they turn responsively to him. Such response is grounded in God's redemptive judgment in history, however, and does not proceed automatically apart from chastening experiences. Stated otherwise, when the Lord has finished with Israel, Israel is responsive.

Both the Lord and Israel are described in animal figures. The Lord roars "like a lion" (v. 10) suggesting the majesty, power, ferocity, and commanding role associated with the lion. From every direction there is response to the Lord's roar—from the west, from Egypt, and from Assyria. Israel comes eagerly "like birds . . . and like doves" (v. 11). As a consequence of Israel's response the Lord "will return them to their homes" (v. 11). The phrase suggests the reality of exile. But it is appropriate to any departure from the Lord. Only when people respond "eagerly" (v. 11) to the Lord's overture is return to their former state possible. But when people are responsive, the Lord is quick to bring renewal and restoration. For this is the way of love. In its own time and way, love always triumphs. <u>Love always has the last word.</u>

In summary, Hosea answers this fundamental question: "How do I love thee? Let me count the ways": I love you when I call you into my family and you keep on seeking other gods (vv. 1-2). I love you when I care for you, and you never stop to recognize who it is who takes you by the hand, or heals, or has compassion, or lifts the load when the way becomes weary (vv. 3-4). I love you when your rebellion prompts me to give you up to your own ways (vv. 5-7). I love you when I am distressed in the deep of my heart with a compassion that grows warm and tender, distressed at the prospect of giving you up, my son (vv. 8-9). I love you with a patience and a determination that uses all the disciplinary forces of history to bring you back to me, for, whatever the cost, I will not give up on you until my love triumphs (vv. 10-12).

10

Herding the Wind

12:1-14

There are few figures of speech more descriptive of absolute futility than that formulated by Hosea: "Ephraim herds the wind, and pursues the east wind all the day long" (12:1). One may herd a flock of sheep or cattle on the field; even wild animals on the plain. But to "herd the wind" is the apex of futility. The same word is used in other contexts to describe the normal work of a herdsman, but here it is used metaphorically to characterize sheer impossibility and folly. A similar expression is used concerning man's inability to discover abiding satisfaction through the multiplication of his possessions. Having enumerated various attempts he had made to find fulfillment through the accumulation of possessions, the Preacher of Ecclesiastes summed up his endeavors by saying, "Then I considered all that my hands had done and the toil I had spent in doing it, and behold, all was vanity and a striving after the wind" (Eccl. 2:11).

Toward what action was Israel's futility directed? What was so graphically characterized as "herding the wind"? Verse 1 suggests that Israel's futile attempt to save themselves through international politics is the focus of the prophet's concern: "They make a bargain with Assyria, and oil is carried to Egypt" (v. 1). Yet, this same sense of futility extended beyond that specific concern, reaching to all of the actions described in chapter 12. The whole of Israel's action was well characterized as attempting to "herd the wind" to "pursue the east wind" (v. 1). Their futile attempt to save themselves (11:12 to 12:1) their possible failure to follow the example of Jacob (12:2-6), their false sense of security which displaced reliance upon the Lord (12:7-9), their forsaking the revelation of God (12:10-14)—each of these separate actions was as foolish and as idiotic as attempting to herd the wind, to pursue the east wind.

I. Betraying the Lord and Seeking to Save One's Self, 12:1

The verse division between chapters 11 and 12 in the Hebrew text occurs at 11:11; verse 12 marking the first verse of chapter 12 in the Hebrew Bible. There is a change of emphasis with 11:12 which focuses on Ephraim's betrayal of the Lord. The whole of 11:12 to 12:1 focuses on the futility of betrayal. Betraying the Lord in order to secure one's future through some other means, foreign alliances in this instance, is as futile as trying to "herd the wind."

"Lies" and "deceit" formed the context of Israel's betrayal of the Lord.[1] The word translated "lies" is not the common word for "lying." Of five occurrences with this connotation, three are in Hosea, one in Nahum 3:1, and another in Psalm 59:12. The RSV translates the same word as "treachery" in Hosea 7:3 and as "lies" in 10:13. The root verb from which the noun is derived means to be disappointing, to deceive, to fail. The connotation is clarified by its parallel usage with "deceit." "Deceit" is associated with treachery and derives from a verb which means to beguile or to deal treacherously with another. The point is clear. Israel's guilt reached far beyond falsehood, although that would have been a severe breach of relationship within covenant faith. Israel had acted deceptively, betraying the Lord, acting treacherously. Such an attitude was isolated by Hosea in another context: "They turn to Baal; they are like a treacherous [a word directly related to "deceit, v. 12] bow," (7:16).

The futility of betraying the Lord, of multiplying "falsehood and violence" and seeking to ensure their own national identity through alliances with Assyria and Egypt was as foolish and as purposeless as herding the wind or pursuing the east wind (v. 1). The word translated "east wind" is often used as the violent and scorching wind from the desert on the southeast; the sirocco. Such a wind is violent and destructive: ". . . his fierce blast in the day of the east wind" (Isa. 27:8). It was a mysterious entity, far from the understanding of a person like Job: "What is the way to the place

---

[1] Wolff interprets "me" as a reference to the prophet, not to God. *op. cit.,* p. 209.

. . . where the east wind is scattered upon the earth" (Job 38:24). How ridiculous, that Israel should attempt to pursue the "east wind," scorching, powerful, and hidden in mystery. Man's betrayal of God is no less foolish than this ridiculous action; whatever the generation, wherever the event, whoever the people.

II. Following the Example of Jacob, Israel's Ancestor, 12:2-6

Hosea specifies the Lord's indictment of Israel (v. 2) and follows this by an example of the way in which repentant Israel may find life and renewal (vv. 3-6). To fail to follow this example would be as foolish as attempting to "herd the wind."

First, although specification of specific charges is lacking, Hosea brings the Lord's indictment against both Judah and Israel: "The Lord has an indictment" (v. 2). The word for "indictment" (*riv*) is identical to that in Hosea 4:1 and suggests the common "lawsuit" motif in Old Testament literature. Specific charges are not catalogued, but logic suggests that the treachery of 11:12, the falsehood and violence of 12:1, coupled with the overtures to Assyria and Egypt (v. 1) are adequate grounds for suggesting that the Lord "will punish Jacob . . . requite him according to his deeds" (v. 2).

Second, the action of the patriarch Jacob offers an appropriate model for repentance and renewal (vv. 3-6). Hosea had introduced "Jacob" as a synonym for Israel (v. 2), and in that context, he now illustrates how Israel of his own generation might well follow the example of the patriarch.

The essential pattern is clear: Jacob was deceptive with his brother (cf. Gen. 25:27 ff; 27:1 ff) and was presumptive to the point that he strove with God. Although Jacob prevailed over the figure with whom he wrestled at Peniel (Gen. 32:22 ff) there was also a sense in which Jacob himself was overcome. For the Lord was the victor: "He wept and sought his favor" (v. 4). On an earlier occasion, Jacob "met God at Bethel, and there God spoke with him" (v. 4). So, Jacob the trickster, the supplanter who deceived his brother on two distinct occasions (cf. Gen. 27:36) met the Lord and in meeting him, he wept and sought the Lord's favor (v. 4). The struggles of Jacob,

his transformation from "Jacob" to "Israel" (cf. Gen. 32:27-28) together become a model for all those whose lives are marred by
comparable deceit and treachery (cf. 11:12).

On the basis of Jacob's example, Hosea encourages Israel to do
three things "by the help of your God." *First*, return to the Lord.
The word "return" is directly related to the word "repent." Man's
first need, whether in ancient Israel or in contemporary society,
is a return to the Lord. *Second*, "Hold fast to love and justice."
The word translated "hold fast" means to guard or keep. "Love"
is the word for covenant love, often translated in the RSV as "steadfast
love." It is a quality of love uniquely related to covenant living;
that love which prompts faithfulness to the relationships created
by the covenant. "Justice" is grounded in the decrees of God and
suggests the whole of his revelation as it pertains to the ordered
life of covenant living. *Third*, "wait continually for your God." The
word translated "wait" *(qawah)* is the verb from which one of the
words for hope is derived. To hope in the Old Testament is to wait
patiently on the Lord. This does not suggest a passive, do-nothing
attitude. But it does suggest that biblical hope is grounded in God,
the finality of the outcome being assured by him. The focus of hope
is in the action of God within history; action which includes man's
creative involvement, but which is not limited to man's potential.

III. The False Sense of Security That Displaces Reliance upon the Lord, 12:7-9

The affluence of the eighth century B.C. (cf. 10:1 ff) lead Israel
to a false sense of security which obscured the fact that the land
which was the gift of God could be taken from them (vv. 8-9).

First, Hosea *designated* Israel as "a trader, in whose hands are
false balances" (v. 7). The word translated "a trader" may also be
translated "Canaan"; suggesting a note of derision. Israel had become
that which she was to have displaced. Although translators generally
translate the word as a trader or merchant (NEB), the Jerusalem
Bible translates "Canaan" with the suggestion that it is used disparag-
ingly for Israel, "infected by the spirit of commercialism charac-

teristic of the people whom he has supplanted" (cf. JB, Hosea 12:7).
"False" balances are deceitful (the same word is translated "deceit"
in 11:12).

That deceitful weights and measures were a continuing problem
in Israel is suggested by numerous demands for "righteous weights;
righteous in the sense that they conform to the norm established
for them; (cf. Amos 8:5; Lev. 19:35 ff; Deut. 25:13 ff; Prov. 20:10).
Such a deceptive trader, a "Canaan," "loves to oppress"—oppression
is not a forced option!

Second, Israel's defense consists of pride which has overrun itself
to the point of arrogance (v. 8). "Success" is a prime defense—the
end justifies the means: "I am rich" might well be translated "I
have prospered" (with an appropriate emphasis on wealth). The NEB
translates this: "Surely I have become a rich man, I have made my
fortune." The double phrase "But I am rich, I have gained wealth
for myself" suggests parallel but slightly distinct emphases.

The text is somewhat confusing at the close of verse 8. Translators
generally follow the same essential meaning as does the RSV: "All
his riches can never offset the guilt he has incurred." But following
the Hebrew text rather closely, one might translate this phrase: "[in]
all my labors they will not find me [guilty of] iniquity and sin."
This suggests a protestation of innocence by the accused, as irrational
as the protestation may be. One is reminded of the church at Laodi-
cea." "For you say, I am rich, I have prospered, and I need nothing;
not knowing that you are wretched, pitiable, poor, blind, and naked"
(Rev. 3:17). To protest innocence in the face of evidence adduced
by the prophet is to compound the guilt of Israel, adding to their
evil deeds a callousness which precludes recognition of guilt.

Third, the Lord will restore Israel to a state of homelessness like
she knew before receiving the gift of the land (v. 9). During the
fall festival, the feast of tabernacles, people dwelt in tents during
the festival. This may have been partially functional, providing
temporary housing; but it was far more symbolic, suggesting those
days when Israel dwelt without land and established houses. Hosea's
point is clear, the Lord will make Israel a homeless people in the
future as once they were in the past.

IV. Forsaking the Revelation of God, 12:10-14

Although the Lord revealed himself to Israel through a variety
of media (v. 10), his revelation was rejected in equally varied ways
(vv. 11-14). Rejection of the revealed will of God is as ridiculous
as attempting to "herd the wind" or to catch the "east wind." Such
rejection of the Lord's revelation was further evidence of Israel's
deception and betrayal.

First, revelation comes in a variety of forms; including word, vision,
and parable (v. 10). The certainty and clarity of revelation for the
people of God is underscored by Hosea. The Lord revealed himself
by *speaking* to the prophets (*dibarti*). The word (*dabar*) is a common
medium for the *revelation* of God. It is a *creative* event, as suggested
by the theme of creation by the word in Genesis 1. The word also
carries within itself the *power* of its own fulfillment; it is a dynamic
event (cf. Isa. 55:10). Also, the word describes a time of *meeting*
with the Lord. When the prophets spoke of the "Word of the Lord"
as having come to them, they described their own experience of
God's dynamic *presence* in creative power. The word was an *event*,
a happening, a time of meeting between the prophet and the Lord,
between the people and the Lord.

Also, the Lord revealed himself through "vision"; those ecstatic,
uplifted moments when the prophets were inspired to see beyond
the normal range of events and circumstances. Prophets like Isaiah,
for example, identified their messages with the "vision": "The vision
of Isaiah, the son of Amoz, which he saw . . ." (Isa. 1:1; cf. Ezek.
1:1; Obad. 1:1). The Lord also revealed himself through parables,
as in the case of Isaiah's parable of the vineyard (Isa. 5:1 ff) or
the parable which Nathan told David (cf. 2 Sam. 12:1 ff). The word
translated as a noun, "parables" is actually a verb which can be
translated, "I make likenesses, or comparisons." Hence, the word
should not be limited to parables as a specific literary form. Rather,
one might think in the broader sense of comparisons or similitudes
(parables, symbols, etc).

The varied means whereby the Lord reveals himself suggests that
interpreters should take into consideration the particular form repre-

sented in a passage before seeking to interpret the passage. Is one interpreting a passage concerned with history? Is one dealing with parabolic material? Is the material visionary in nature? No passage of Scripture should be interpreted without seeking to determine the precise literary form represented.

Second, in view of the Lord's revelation, one may be sure that rebellion and ingratitude will be punished (v. 11). Because of Gilead's iniquity, the inhabitants of that region will come to "nothingness," just as the altars of Gilgal shall become "stone heaps on the furrows of the field" (v. 11) because of false worship represented in the sacrifice of bulls at that shrine. Those who reject the revelation of the Lord's will can expect the reality of judgment within history.

Third, the people of God are to live with the priority of the prophetic word. The purpose of Hosea in vv. 12 ff. is to focus on the priority of the prophetic word and its creative power over the static relationships represented in the patriarchs. In contrasting Jacob (v. 12) and Moses (v. 13), Hosea asserts the priority of the prophet; whose revelatory word he has already emphasized (v. 10). Israel's hope rests in the prophetic word, comparable to the prophet Moses who lead Israel out of Egypt.

Perhaps by the time of Hosea, there were competitive attitudes concerning the promises of a land associated with the patriarch and the Exodus emphases which stressed the contingent nature of covenant life; covenant and law being interlocked. While Hosea stops short of disclaiming the patriarch Jacob; his portrayal in verse 12 is less than commendable. A Hebrew becomes an indentured servant who tends sheep for a wife! Such a picture was far removed from the picture of a deliverer like Moses (v. 13). In essence, the hope of the people of God rests not in a promise made long ago concerning a land; it rests in positive response to the dynamic, creative word of the prophet uttered in the immediacy of one's own trials and crises. Perhaps it was because Ephraim failed to respond to that prophetic word that Hosea concluded by affirming that the Lord will "turn his blood-guilt up him, and will turn back upon him his reproaches" (v. 14).

11

There Is No Other!

13:1-16

Biblical religion commends a spirit of tolerance with regard to the convictions which others may cherish and profess. Such a conception of tolerance focuses on attitudes of patience and respect for the personhood of all individuals. Consequently, the use of material violence in support of faith is a course of action beyond which the community of faith has long since passed in its historical pilgrimage. Christian faith commends particular connotations of tolerance toward persons of other races, social strata, nationalities, and religious persuasions.

Yet there remains a sense in which biblical religion is from one perspective intolerant; as intolerant as truth, or righteousness, or justice. Just as a finely machined part for a delicate instrument must have as small a degree of tolerance as the machinist is capable of producing, so in areas of faith there are areas in which biblical faith is "intolerant." In this regard, Emil Brunner once suggested that "truth itself is intolerant." He grounded this statement on the assumption that "the recognition of one truth excludes the possibility of recognizing its opposite to be true as well." Further:

> "If it is true that twice two are four, then it is simply false
> to say that twice two are five or three. If it is true that Julius
> Caesar was murdered on March 15 of the year 44 B.C., then
> it is just false to say that he died a natural death in the year
> 45. Truth is always single and exclusive. If there is only one
> God, then there is not more than one." [1]

---

[1] Emil Brunner, *The Great Invitation and Other Sermons* (Philadelphia: The Westminster Press, 1955), p. 107.

It is in this regard that chapter 13 of Hosea focuses on the theme, "There is no other." With an intolerance born of the nature of truth, the prophet insisted that for Israel "besides me there is no savior" (v. 4). This broad theme may in turn be extended to the entire chapter: for the community of faith there is no other glory than that conceived in relationship with the Lord (vv. 1-3), no other savior (vv. 4-8), no other king (vv. 9-11), and no other hope (vv. 12-16).

I. No Other Glory, 13:1-3

Hosea consistently laments the "lost glory" of Israel. Departure from the Lord means that "Ephraim's glory shall fly away like a bird" (9:11), or, "its glory which has departed from it" (10:5). While Hosea does not use the word "glory" in 13:1-3, he does deal with one facet of that basic concept; namely, the exaltation of Israel among the nations. These verses (vv. 1-3) form a judgment speech, composed of both the statement of motivation (vv. 1-2) and the verdict (v. 3).

First, prior exaltation is replaced by rebellion against the Lord (vv. 1-2). There was a time of such prominence for Israel that when he spoke "men trembled." He was "exalted." Ephraim once had such prominence among the tribes of Israel. But Ephraim had long since ceased to exist as a tribe. Hosea probably used Ephraim to denote Mt. Ephraim, where the royal residence was located.

It is difficult to determine what precise period of history may have been in the prophet's mind, but whatever the period, he referred to the relative prominence which Israel achieved within the complex of international events of the ancient world. Or, he may have in mind the prior prominence of Ephraim within the tribal confederacy and the way in which present Ephraim (the Northern Kingdom) has lost that position of influence. In any event, Hosea indicates that through the worship of Baal, Ephraim "incurred guilt" and "died." Trapped by the attractions of Baalism, Ephraim of Hosea's day multiplied their sin, they made calf images (v. 2) and incorporated them into worship, sacrificing to them and kissing them (apparently reflecting some aspect of Canaanite ritual).

Second, in keeping with "judgment speeches" generally, Hosea concludes with the verdict. "Therefore" is a common means of introducing the verdict in prophetic speeches of judgment. The essential characteristic of the verdict is that of temporality; the fleeting, temporary nature of the nation. Israel is characterized as "morning mist," "the dew that goes early away," "chaff that swirls from the threshing floor," "smoke from a window" (3). Apart from the Lord and his purposes, there is no permanence.

An appropriate sense of glory, which suggests stability and well-being, is directly related to one's relationship with the Lord. There was a time in Israel when she knew such glory; she was exalted (v. 1). Through compromised theology and worship (v. 2), she forfeited that glory and was destined to become a transient, homeless people; without national identity, wanderers who are as insecure and temporal as the morning mist or dew, as the chaff on the threshing floor, or the smoke from a house (v. 3).

II. No Other Savior, 13:4-8

For Israel there was no other savior than the Lord who redeemed them out of Egypt and cared for them in the wilderness. They had experienced no other god than the Lord. His redemptive activity was responsible for their deliverance. Hosea indicts Israel for having forgotten this (vv. 4-6), and in his verdict (vv. 7-8), describes the destruction of the nation precipitated by forgetting the Lord.

First, the uniqueness of the Lord's salvation (vv. 4,5) is soon forgotten in the midst of the abundance of his gifts (v. 6). There are two facets to the prophet's indictment. It was the Lord alone who redeemed Israel; Israel had forgotten his redemptive grace.

"I am the Lord your God" is uniquely associated with the Exodus experience and suggests the uniqueness of the Lord (especially the phrase "I am the Lord", *'ani YHWH*). The phrase "I am the Lord" is a way of affirming the singular nature of God; the fact that he alone exists as subject, before whom all else is object. He is the only real God.[2]

---

[2] Cf. Roy L. Honeycutt, "Exodus," *The Broadman Bible Commentary*, Vol. I, (Nashville: Broadman Press, 1969), p. 369.

The word "know" in Old Testament literature suggests personal, experiential knowledge. It is in this context that Hosea suggests that Israel knew no god but the Lord (v. 4) and that the Lord "knew" Israel in the wilderness (v. 5). There was an interlocking, personal relationship between Israel and the Lord which flowed in both directions: from Israel to the Lord, and from the Lord to Israel. The uniqueness of this relationship is unquestionable, as affirmed by the prophet: "Besides me there is no savior." "Savior" might be translated deliverer, from a verb meaning to deliver or save. It is the same word from which Joshua, Hosea, and Jesus are derived. The word always had "spiritual" connotations since the Lord was related to the whole of life, including health, national well-being, deliverance in times of battle or other crises. It does not, however, have the restricted connotation that "salvation" currently has for some. The breadth of the word is suggestive of the manner in which the Lord "delivers" from *varied* situations.

The essential characteristic of Hosea's indictment relates to the way in which "they forgot me." To "forget" involves more than a lapse of memory. It has to do with more active concepts of renunciation; even of apostasy, as in the case of "forgetting" the Lord and turning to Baal. The biblical writer cautions Israel about forgetting the goodness of God following the Exodus-wilderness experience:

> "And when the Lord your God brings you into the land . . . with great and goodly cities, which you did not build, and houses full of all good things, which you did not fill, and cisterns hewn out, which you did not hew, and vineyards and olive trees, which you did not plant, and when you eat and are full, *then take heed lest you forget the Lord*" (Deut. 6:10-12).

Second, the verdict upon those who forget the Lord is stated in destructive terminology. Technically, the Lord is described in theriomorphic terms. He is described with similes such as the lion, leopard, and bear. The picture is graphic and clear. Within historical events of the latter third of the eighth century B.C., Israel is decimated, finally destroyed. The uniqueness of Israel's relationship to the Lord was the foundational premise on which the whole of her existence was built. Her glory rested in the Lord. Her salvation from bondage was brought about by him. Removed from him, there was neither glory nor salvation; only destruction and annihilation.

III. No Other King, 13:9-11

Was Hosea opposed to kingship as an institution; following the antimonarchial mood of Samuel (1 Sam. 8:6,9-18)? Or, was Hosea opposed only to kingship as it had developed in his century? The answer to this is difficult if not impossible to establish beyond question. But this is obvious: Hosea was opposed to kingship stripped of charismatic power related to the presence of God. Verses 9-11 form a "disputation" or argumentative speech; one in which the prophet speaks for God and enters into argument with the people.

Where now, the Lord argues, are your king and your princes "those of whom you said, 'Give me a king and princes' " (cf. 1 Sam. 8:6,9-18). The suggestion is subtle but relatively clear. Abandoning the Lord, Israel sought kings and princes. Israel moved from theocracy to monarchy. Where has this led the nation, if not to destruction (v. 9); who, indeed, "can help you"? Or, the prophet may have in mind the rapid turnover in kingship following the time of Jeroboam II, when six kings reigned in about 15 years; some for a year and less. God gave them "in my anger," and took them "away in my wrath" (v. 11).

Because of the sin of relying upon kings of their own making, rather than the Lord, judgment is sure. Hosea speaks of the results of Israel's iniquity as "bound up," "kept in store" (v. 12). Her judgment is likened to a child who waits only for the birthpangs of childbirth to come forth, however reluctantly (v. 13). Each of these figures of speech is intended to suggest that the judgment of the nation is inevitable—it is bound up in history, waiting only to be delivered. Ultimately, there is no king but the Lord, and those who turn to others find that their judgment is bound up in their historical fate.

IV. No Other Hope, 13:12-16

This is a "divine saying"; one in which the prophet speaks in the first person for the Lord: "Shall I ransom them from the power of Sheol?" (v. 14). Man's hope rests in the action of God. He alone is able to ransom from Sheol and death. What is to be the verdict? First, perhaps it should be said that the verdict is not established arbitrarily. It is grounded in the response which Israel has made to the Lord. Second, whether it is to be life or death for a people depends upon their relationship to the Lord: "See, I have set before you this day life and good, death and evil" (Deut. 30:15).

From the Hebrew text, it is impossible to determine whether verse 14 should be read as an interrogative or as an indicative. The King James translation follows the indicative: "I will ransom them." The larger context suggests a negative response on the part of the Lord. For example, "compassion is hid from my eyes" (v. 14, RSV). The NEB translates the phrase, "I will put compassion out of my sight." The Jerusalem Bible translates the passage, "I have no eyes for pity." This negative mood suggests the interrogative, "Shall I . . ."; together with a negative answer.

The answer to the questions of Sheol and death is, "No!" The Lord will neither ransom nor redeem. Rather, he calls for the plagues of death and the destruction of Sheol (14). There is no hope for those who abandon the Lord, substituting idols for the reality of God's presence, compromising faith with other religions, rebelling against the Lord, relying on their kings to the exclusion of the Lord. For such persons, there is no hope.

As a further illustration of the hopelessness of man apart from the redeeming power of the Lord, Hosea utilizes another figure of speech; that of the reed plant. It may flourish for a period of time, but ultimately the storm wind, the "east wind" commonly identified as the "Sirroco" will blow in from the desert, dry up the moisture, and destroy the reed (v. 15). Samaria has rebelled against God and must bear her guilt: "They shall fall by the sword, their little ones shall be dashed in pieces, and their pregnant women ripped open" (v. 16). Again, for rebellious, unrepentant persons, there is no hope apart from the Lord.

12

The Long Way Home
14:1-9

The way back to the Lord, to repentance and the renewal of covenant life, often involves "the long way home." There are no short-cuts to dynamic relationships with the Lord. For Hosea's generation, as for Gomer, the "long way home" involved periods of discipline and deprivation, moments of desolation and despair, experiences of futility and loneliness, times of repentance and renewal. The way back is never so easy as it may seem to some, for the simple reason that we wander so far from God. We litter the path leading away from the Lord with the broken fragments of our relationships. While the way back may not be easy, we may be sure that it is certain.

It is to those who stand afar off, separated and removed from the Lord's purposes that the prophet addresses his closing appeal. For every believer, troubled over both his estrangement from the Lord and the quality of his present commitment and discouraged at the level of his achievement as a disciple, the words of the prophet are encouraging. There is a way back to God, a way out of one's present predicament, a way beyond the level of one's present achievement. The call is personal, urgent, and pertinent.

Four words form the structure of this salvation oracle, a proclamation grounded in the basic assumption that salvation grows out of God's free love shared with needy believers.[1]

---

[1] Cf. Roy L. Honeycutt, "Hosea," *The Broadman Bible Commentary*, Vol. 7 (Nashville: Broadman Press, 1972), pp. 58 ff. I have sought to avoid direct usage of material found in the Commentary, but I am convinced that this four-fold emphasis remains valid for chapter 14.

I. The Wanderer, 14:1

The appeal to return is grounded in the assumption that the people of God have "stumbled." "Return" is identical to the word translated "repent," and in this instance "repentance" constitutes the focus of the prophetic appeal. This is the necessary point of beginning for every weary wanderer: return! Yet the appeal presupposes a need. "To stumble" is often used in the Old Testament as a way of describing those who have missed the way which God would have them walk: "But my people have forgotten me, they burn incense to false gods; they have stumbled in their ways" (Jer. 18:15; cf. Isa. 3:8; 59:10). Hosea himself used the figure of speech on half a dozen occasions to describe Israel's failure.

Like a person who stumbles beneath a heavy burden, so the people of God stumbled beneath the burden of their iniquity. Or, to shift analogies, their iniquity became an obstacle in their path, causing them to stumble. Whatever the specific overtones of the figure of speech, the cause for stumbling is our sin. Our separation from God involves more than a minor deviation from the right way, more than a slight error of direction on our course. Let no one be mistaken; let no one make excuse. Separation from both the Lord and those qualities of life related to the community of faith is the direct consequence of our sin. The fundamental seriousness of sin is the fact of separation. Sin separates persons from God, from one another. Even internally, sin separates individuals within so that we are no longer whole persons. People who know this quality of estrangement and separation need wholeness more than anything else: wholeness with God, with other persons, within one's own self. Fundamentally, the purposes of God in salvation relate to wholeness: bringing together in the wholeness of time persons who have been separated in time.

II. The Way, 14:2-3

What is the way back to the Lord; to the purposes of his will for us? Response to so profound an issue is liable to the charge of superficiality, if it proceeds from our own wisdom alone. Fortunately, we are not left to the guidance of our own best wisdom. The prophet isolates three aspects of the way back to the Lord.

First, the way back to the Lord presupposes appropriate *confession:* "Take with you words and return to the Lord" (v. 2). For most of us there are some things that we need to say to the Lord. "Confession" as traditionally described in both the New Testament and in the community of faith, the church, is significant. Putting faith into words, acknowledging guilt, asking forgiveness; each of these and other aspects of religious experience not only *need* to be verbalized, they *must* be cast into word-form if they are to become real. To be sure you will have to form the words for yourself, but there is something that each of us ought to be saying to the Lord: "Take with you words" (v. 2).

Some may object by observing that we live in a time when the multiplicity of words and the conflict between words and deeds have combined to make language suspect. One finds extreme expressions of this, as in the assumption that "words don't matter." Frankly, through the constant barrage of various media and the hypocrisy of the seventies, language has lost many of its impelling qualities. We have suffered from an overexposure of language. Especially have national political scandals called words into question; we have experienced the generation of the big lie.

But words are fundamentally important. Human existence comes to reality through language, through words. Without words, we could not communicate so well as we might. Our ideas would never escape the prison of our own minds. Creativity would be stultified. Our personalities could never come to full expression without words. The whole of man does come to being in language; in word-event. So let us not succumb to the idea that it does not matter whether or not we verbalize our faith. We need to *say* something about faith experience.

Second, the way back to the Lord presupposes an appropriate *content* to what we say to the Lord: "say to him . . ." (v. 2). We not only need to say "something" (as suggested above), Hosea is specific concerning what we need to say to the Lord. While this is not intended as a mechanical speech to be repeated with meaningless repetition by future generations, it does offer believers of every era an appropriate model. Those who have wandered away from the Lord should ask that the Lord take away their iniquity (v. 2). This is the obstacle that separates. Our problem is not our understanding or lack of understanding, although this is not unimportant. Sin is our problem. Our first need is for forgiveness and reconciliation: "Take away all iniquity."

Also, we need to ask that God will "accept that which is good" (v. 2). Israel had "spurned the good" (8:3). Now they are to ask that God accept the "good"; that is, those qualities of covenant living which are so well summarized as the "good." Micah later used the same expression to summarize the whole of God's demand: "He has showed you, O man, what is good" (Mic. 6:8).

Finally, take the praise of your lips to the Lord: "We will render the fruit of our lips" (v. 2). The Hebrew text reads, literally, "bulls of our lips," perhaps suggesting sacrifice of our lips. What better sacrifice than the praise of the Lord? Those whose lips previously had kissed the idolatrous calf associated with Canaanite Baalism (cf. 13:2), now pledge to render their lips to the Lord.

Third, the way back to the Lord presupposes an appropriate *commitment* to him: "Assyria shall not save us" (v. 3). Primary among Israel's sins that separated her from the Lord was putting trust in foreign alliances rather than in the Lord. Dependence upon sources of power and strength other than the Lord effectually separated Israel from the Lord; bringing about, in the process, the national destruction which she had sought to avert.

If the wanderer is to return, there must be an affirmation of faith commitment to the Lord as the strength of life. For Israel, this was achieved by affirming that no longer will they depend upon Assyria. No longer will they depend upon the cavalry (Cf., "we will not ride upon horses," v. 3). No longer will they trust in their idols, "the work of our hands." In essence, when people place their confidence in the Lord as the source of ultimate strength and deliverance, there is a way back home. Apart from the Lord, Israel was like a helpless orphan; the epitome of weakness and need. But an orphan can find strength in the Lord; hence, the prophet's statement, "In thee the orphan finds mercy."

III. The Witness, 14:4-8

The prophet bears witness to three characteristics of the wanderer's return.

First, the return of the wanderer is grounded in the nature of
God (v. 4). As Hosea suggested earlier, viewed from a human point
of view, the Lord would obliterate his people, and the primary reason
for his grace rests in the fact that "I am God, and not man" (Hos.
11:9). God acts as he does because of who he is.

It is the Lord who will "heal their faithlessness" (v. 4). Again,
the seriousness of sin is stressed. Sin is an illness, a malady that
requires healing. Against this background, biblical writers portray
the Lord as a physician who heals his people. For example, Isaiah
spoke of "The day when the Lord binds up the hurt of his people,
and heals the wounds inflicted by his blow" (Isa. 30:26). More specifically related to sin, and the present statement of Hosea, is Jeremiah's
observation: "Return, O faithless sons, I will heal your faithlessness"
(Jer. 3:22; cf. 30:17).

Not only so, God loves continuously (participal) and does so
"freely." There is a freeness in God's love which should not be
confused with cheapness, but which should be affirmed in its own
right. Return to the Lord is based upon his unmerited favor. Who
would take back an adulterous wife (3:1 ff) or a rebellious son
(11:1 ff)—apart from unmerited grace and love? Love creates re-
sponses which otherwise would never come to realization. Man does
not respond with such grace by nature, but God does; and the nearer
we are to the heart of God, the more likely we are to respond
with kindred acts of grace and love toward other persons.

Second, the return of the wanderer reveals varied aspects of the
attributes of both God and man (vv. 5-7). In figures of speech drawn
from the beauty of both field and forest, Hosea described the Lord's
action and man's response. The Lord will be "as the dew to Israel"
(v. 5): Bringing moisture and life, the dew was all the more significant
in a semi-arid land than in a land of abundant rainfall. In an agrarian
society like Israel's, what better way to describe the glory and beauty

of the relationship of the redeemed than with agricultural figures of speech? The absolute reality of one's relationship with God defies precise delineation. One can only describe it through varied figures of speech. When the wanderer returns "he shall blossom as the lily . . . strike root as the poplar" (v. 5). His life is like the fragrance associated with Lebanon, his beauty like the olive (v. 6). At such a time of return and restoration the wanderers will "dwell beneath my shadow"; "they shall blossom as the vine, their fragrance shall be like the wine of Lebanon" (v. 7).

Third, the return of the wanderer will be a time of new attraction (v. 8). No longer attracted to idols, Israel will come to recognize that the Lord has nothing to do with idols. God does not reveal himself through the rigid forms of idols, but in his living word.[2] It is the Lord, not Baal (cf. Hos. 2:8 ff) who will "answer and look after you." Like an evergreen cypress, symbolizing life and vitality, the Lord is the source of life for Israel; not a sacred grove of trees or a sacred post, both of which were associated with pagan forms of worship. It is from the Lord that your fruit comes (v. 8); not from the local baals (cf. 2:8 ff). Those who wander learn through the bitter discipline of experience that it is the Lord who provides sources of healing, sustenance, and purpose. When they return to the Lord, they do so with a new affection, with a new attraction for their lives. Sources of false trust are no longer attractive to those who have been reconciled.

IV. The Wise, 14:9

In a closing verse which is properly understood as applying to the whole of the book, wisdom is associated with understanding and discerning, knowing that "the ways of the Lord are right, and the upright walk in them, but transgressors stumble in them" (v. 9). Stated otherwise, it is a wise thing to hear and respond to the Lord's word.

---

[2] Cf. the polemic against idolatry, based on the nature of revelation in Deuteronomy 4:9 ff.